fc

TRA ...ENCE.

Tr...NSFORMATION.

Formatio books from InterVarsity Press follow the rich tradition of the church in the journey of spiritual formation. These books are not merely about being informed, but about being transformed by Christ and conformed to his image. Formatio stands in InterVarsity Press's evangelical publishing tradition by integrating God's Word with spiritual practice and by prompting readers to move from inward change to outward witness. InterVarsity Press uses the chambered nautilus for Formatio, a symbol of spiritual formation because of its continual spiral journey outward as it moves from its center. We believe that each of us is made with a deep desire to be in God's presence. Formatio books help us to fulfill our deepest desires and to become our true selves in light of God's grace.

SOULS IN FULL SAIL

A CHRISTIAN SPIRITUALITY

FOR THE LATER YEARS

EMILIE GRIFFIN

IVP Books

An imprint of InterVarsity Press
Downers Grove, Illinois

InterVarsity Press
P.O. Box 1400, Downers Grove, IL 60515-1426
World Wide Web: www.ivpress.com
E-mail: email@ivpress.com

InterVarsity Press® is the book-publishing division of InterVarsity Christian Fellowship/USA®, a movement of
students and faculty active on campus at hundreds of universities, colleges and schools of nursing in the United
States of America, and a member movement of the International Fellowship of Evangelical Students. For
information about local and regional activities, write Public Relations Dept., InterVarsity Christian
Fellowship/USA, 6400 Schroeder Rd., P.O. Box 7895, Madison, WI 53707-7895, or visit the IVCF website
at <www.intervarsity.org>.

All Scripture quotations, unless otherwise indicated, are taken from the Jerusalem Bible, copyright ©1966 by
Darton, Longman & Todd, Ltd. and Doubleday & Company, Inc. All rights reserved.

Grateful acknowledgment is made to Praying and Hosanna magazines, in which portions of this material
appeared in slightly different form. Some portions of this book previously appeared in the author's work
Homeward Voyage, © 1994 by Emilie Griffin.

Design: Cindy Kiple
Images: Alison Langley/Getty Images

ISBN 978-0-8308-3548-5

Printed in the United States of America ∞

Library of Congress Cataloging-in-Publication Data

Griffin, Emilie.
  Souls in full sail: a Christian spirituality for the later years /
Emilie Griffin.
    p. cm.
  ISBN 978-0-8308-3548-5 (pbk.: alk. paper)
  1. Older people—Religious life. 2. Aging—Religious
aspects—Christianity. 3. Spirituality. I. Title.
  BV4580.G75 2010
  248.8'5—dc22
                                                                2010033187

P	16	15	14	13	12	11	10	9	8	7	6	5	4	3	2	1
Y	24	23	22	21	20	19	18	17	16	15	14	13	12	11		

For William

and for Lucy, Ardis and Avery

Henry and Larisa

Sarah and Troy

CONTENTS

PREFACE

On a certain day in June 1993, I realized that my life was about to change. Radically. It was the first or second day of June, a weekday, and my husband, William Griffin, and I, both writers, had been invited to address a women's group at the Orleans Club (pronounced "Or-lay-on"). This imposing mansion with high steps, on upper St. Charles Avenue in New Orleans, has a full auditorium and a fine complement of refreshments and service. It was an elegant day of blazing sunshine, a successful day in most respects. But my mother wasn't there.

She was eighty-one, and a celebrated person in New Orleans, known as a businesswoman and entrepreneur who had founded three companies and still remained current on the tourism and literary scene. Many people called her "Helen," as I did. Others called her "Mrs. D." Our on-stage presentation was the sort of event she would truly enjoy, and I felt sure (I had talked to her by telephone the night before) that she would be there. When she failed to appear, the morning event went on as scheduled. Various women noticed her absence; she was

a favorite guest at any occasion. My husband and I made light
of her not being there. But I was concerned. I telephoned her,
only to learn that she had had a sequence of seven falls. She had
been unable to get to her front door, let alone to her car.

I moved in with her that day and spent the next year as her
caregiver, assisted by the able and competent Edith Johnson,
who was employed by my mother and us on a full-time basis.
Edith had cared for my grandmother in her last illness. When
my grandmother died in 1979, my mother continued to employ
Edith as a companion and factotum. In 1980, when our family
moved from New York City to New Orleans, Edith Johnson
divided her time between my mother's household and ours. Six
months after the Orleans Club day my mother moved into our
home on Prytania Street, where she remained for another seven
months until she died.

My mother had been in frail health for twelve years. In fact,
my husband and I and our children had moved to New Orleans
because of her. In 1980 she had a brush with death. Because a
concerned doctor made a house call, realized the severity of
the situation and put her into the hospital for a blood transfu-
sion, she survived. And we decided to relocate.

But once we had arrived in New Orleans, my mother, who
was then sixty-eight and the chief executive of three busi-
nesses, seemed to make a marvelous recovery. For a dozen
years, in spite of her disability, she continued with the things
she loved—and being the person we loved.

I was forty-four the year we moved. The move was prompted
by my mother's frailty, but I didn't think of it as a time to focus
on mortality. No, instead I concentrated on our joyful reprieve.
I was grateful for it. I was turning over a new page, opening a
new chapter. I began to redevelop my life in a new setting,

with different objectives. One of these was to cultivate a friend-ship with my mother on renewed terms of enthusiasm. I made new friends, reconnected with old friends. I got to know my husband better. And I tried, while working full time, writing books and studying theology at night, to be a good mother to our three teenage children.

And on the day when my mother couldn't come to the Or-leans Club, I was fifty-six. Twelve years had passed. How was it that I had not known, through more than a decade, that on a certain day, perhaps just a morning, everything would change?

Until then, I had felt that my mother was still in charge, because she still had such a presence and power in all circum-stances. She was old, but who would have guessed it? She had such charm and authority. She radiated all the best qualities of youth and old age. But all at once, almost in one day, it seemed, I was in charge and had to move into high gear to take respon-sibility for her.

Other things were changing as well. Our children—Lucy, Henry and Sarah—had grown up. They were finishing college, choosing their life work. Their lives were becoming disen-gaged from ours. Our work lives were also changing. For a decade I had held salaried positions, both for my mother's firms and for three New Orleans advertising agencies, where I worked as creative director and held executive roles. But now I was self-employed, building a freelance practice and intend-ing to write books, lead retreats and focus on the spiritual life. My husband had been a freelance writer and editor for more than a decade. This new flexibility, I felt, would make sense for the years ahead.

We were getting older, and we knew it. My mother's in-

creasing charm and frailty were mirrors of our future. It was
time to consider not so much the life journey as the end of that
journey. My husband and I had been married for thirty years.
My mother and I seemed to be linked; my husband traveled
with us, but following at a slight distance, like a consort ship.
I knew that his parents had died; no doubt he had already made
the passage that we were making.

THE SEA VOYAGE

So I came to write about the later years, my mother's and my
own. But as a spiritual writer I wanted to interpret the late-in-
life passage for everyone. I wanted to voice my fears about
change and also the strengthening power of the spiritual life.

I began to search for a central metaphor that would convey our
life passage, the stretch just ahead, the later part of the journey.
Something new was happening, starkly different from what had
gone before. It was time to cut loose from what had mattered up
to now. I thought: *It is a voyage, but there is no map, no clear style of
navigation. We have settled, figuratively at least, into our deck chairs; we
have pulled the blankets up against cold and the ocean spray. We are both
the passengers and navigators for this late-in-life adventure.*

Ours is a reading from the book of Wisdom:

Or someone else, taking ship to cross the raging sea,
invokes a log even frailer than the vessel that bears him.
No doubt that ship is the product of a craving for gain,
its building embodies the wisdom of the shipwright,
but your providence, Father, is what steers it,
you have opened a pathway even through the sea,
a safe way over the waves,
showing that you can save, whatever happens,

so that even without skill a man may sail abroad.

It is not your will that the works of your Wisdom lie idle,
and hence men entrust their lives to the smallest piece
of wood,
cross the high seas on a raft and come safe to port.
Why, in the beginning even, while the proud giants
were perishing,
the hope of the world took refuge on a raft
and, steered by your hand, preserved the germ of a new
generation for the ages to come. (Wisdom 14:1-6)

So, I hope to explore a Christian spirituality for the later
years. The metaphor of a sea voyage really suits this uncharted
territory, the uncertainty of what lies ahead. God is my guide
as I steer into the unknown.

CONSIDERING THE HOPE OF HEAVEN

At the same time I mean to examine the Christian hope of
heaven, a promise I believe in. In various chapters I will voice
my doubts and distress at the limitations of this life, the dimin-
ishment of the body and the constrictions of time. Yet I want
to be open with you. I have fully embraced the Christian faith,
with its promises of glory and resurrection. I am writing not to
overthrow or challenge these great teachings but rather to take
hold of them, as C. S. Lewis did, to see them in new ways, to
clothe them in new language and new metaphors.

This book takes for granted the truth of Christianity and its
promises. The wrestling you will find on these pages comes
from my own need to surrender, to come into a place of peace.
I need to accept my own death and the death of those I love.
At the same time I sense a deep joy in existence, a world con-

tinually speaking to me of the blessing of existence, the wonder of the natural world and of beauty in all its expressions.

I write to celebrate the truth of things, not so much by giving answers as by asking questions. I draw clues and inspirations from the Bible, from poets, from the wisdom of my own family and friends, from scholars now and then. As you will soon see, the book does not proceed in a linear way. Sometimes the journey moves forward by raising questions and voicing doubts. Sometimes it comes to a still point, exploring the immediate and present moment. These reflections should be read slowly and prayerfully. At the end of each chapter I suggest some spiritual exercises for the later years. Questions for discussion will follow each chapter.

In behalf of nautical and seagoing metaphors, I offer these words from Virginia Woolf:

> For this is the truth about our soul, . . . our self, who fish-like inhabits deep seas and plies her way among obscurities, threading her way among the boles of giant weeds, over sun-flickered spaces and on and on into gloom, cold, deep, and inscrutable; suddenly she shoots to the surface and sports in the wind-wrinkled waves.

Why have I felt such an attraction to the metaphors of navigation and seagoing journeys? I will explore this too, to the extent that I understand it myself, as these reflections unfold.

Though it draws on personal memories, this book is not quite a memoir. It is an extended meditation, a Christian reflection on getting older. I write these thoughts not as instruction, nor as analysis, but rather as a way of coming to terms with my own history and my future, in hopes that others will also be strengthened for the journey.

On September 9, 2009, I led a discussion for a women's group in Alexandria, Louisiana, which focused on spiritual life. At this September meeting the text in question was C. S. Lewis's sermon "The Weight of Glory," first preached at St. Mary the Virgin Church in Oxford, England, in 1941. As I prepared for the discussion I realized how much Lewis had shaped me over a lifetime. Among many influences, Lewis had been primary. His words and imagination had kindled in me a lively hope of heaven. "The Weight of Glory" does that. I'm not sure quite how. One way is by wrestling with the promises of faith. Lewis questions the old metaphors of the resurrected life. He questions them. Then he embraces them.

During my preparation I thought of another way Lewis has helped me. He had shown me how a lively faith may move from one generation to the next, through mentors and teachers, relatives and friends, spiritual kinfolk, all. Inspired by Lewis's accounts of his own faith life, I write to pass on the tradition as it was given to me, but in the language chiefly of my own generation.

Like Lewis, I was blessed with a love of the "old writers," including George Herbert, John Donne, Henry Vaughan and John Milton. You will see their influence in this book. Also, I cannot fail to mention Mildred Gayler Christian, my professor of English at Newcomb College, Tulane University. She taught me to be unafraid of seventeenth-century spelling and punctuation, entranced by the poetic depth of the metaphysical poets, challenged by the richness of *Paradise Lost*, by the height of Milton's imagination and the sweep of his narrative line. Reading deeply in the old texts, I was enlivened by the faith of an earlier time and wondered how and when the fire of it would skip over the chasm of centuries to us. Ultimately I saw how

important these writings remain. I am fearless about quoting
them now and again. This book reflects my own twenty-first-
century faith and the influence of those older writers who remain pervasively influential in our time.

Since 1993, when some of these reflections were first written, I have myself been navigating the later years.

MY MOTHER'S DEATH

Probably the most significant event was my mother's death in
July 1994. No matter how much I had anticipated this change,
the blow hit me hard. I must have supposed that if I had tried
a little harder, cared for her a little bit better, she would not
have died. I had a hard time letting go of her presence in my
life, and the greatest sign of that, I think, was my inner signal
to telephone her every evening. At last, after some years, it
began to fade. But that inner signal was just one evidence of
the closeness we had.

Dr. Howard Russell, who had been her doctor and understood many of my mother's ideas about death, tried to console
me. "I hope you know how well you have done," he said. Just
hours after my mother's death he wanted to praise me for my
strong commitment to her care. His words were comforting,
but not at first. It was years before I could remember them and
accept them.

One thing I remember about her passing: the notes she left
behind with instructions for how we were to mourn. She asked
for a "Gilbert and Sullivan funeral," creatively organized by
the Griffins. What in the world did she mean? How could we
respond to one of her last wishes?

In my view her request for a Gilbert and Sullivan kind of
mourning had something to do with the cheerful confidence of

her faith. It wasn't so much that she loved Gilbert and Sullivan's many light operas. She was sending us a message, to celebrate her life, to be joyful and not saddened by our memories.

During one of several funeral services, our son, Henry, honored her Gilbert and Sullivan request. He made a recording of instrumental Gilbert and Sullivan tunes. And he played it for the assembled mourners. While it was playing he gave a charming recollection of his grandmother and her influence on him. He really captured the high imaginative style of her personality. Everyone was touched.

Since then, our lives have changed. My children have left home and married. My husband and I moved from the house on Prytania Street (often mentioned in these pages) to another house on Cadiz Street in uptown New Orleans. We were dealing with many unforeseen circumstances and lived in the Cadiz Street house less than two years. Within a year, our older daughter, Lucy, invited us to move closer to her in Alexandria, Louisiana, and we accepted gratefully. So we sold the Cadiz Street house and then moved to Curtis Drive in Alexandria.

We have lived a decade in this new location. I have been diagnosed with rheumatoid arthritis, a disease which has slowed me down a bit, but hasn't defeated me. Now I walk more slowly, and I use a cane. But I continue to write, to travel and to speak. I have been grateful for the grace to continue doing the things I love. Especially, I am grateful to my husband, William Griffin, for his constant support. He makes it possible for me to continue in my work and to transcend obstacles of illness to the extent that I can.

"You look great," people tell me. And I believe them.

Some of the reflections in this book were prompted by the impending death of my mother. Others were written later. We have outlived her. Yet her presence and influence remain. Since her passing in 1994, many other, and younger, friends have died. I do not always mention them by name. But they are part of my consciousness—and my need to cling to the Christian hope of heaven.

SOULS IN FULL SAIL

In a very short and very wise book on the spiritual life, *Abandonment to Divine Providence,* I find these riveting words: "The present moment always reveals the presence and the power of God." The author of this small treatise helps me to conceive a spiritual destination: to let the wind of the Holy Spirit carry me forward till my soul is in full sail. How amazing to feel so connected to an eighteenth-century French Jesuit. We are centuries apart but of the same mind. He weaves together a spirituality of the immediate moment with the theme of advancing in the journey. He chooses the figure of a voyage. "Our souls steadily advance, never halting, but sweeping along with every wind." Such a lovely objective: souls in full sail. "Every current," writes Jean Pierre de Caussade, "every technique thrusts us forward in our voyage to the infinite."

I continue in the voyage, looking for a Christian spirituality of the later years.

SETTING OUT

The Surprise of Getting Older

We do not set out to become old. Far from it. We hardly intend even to become middle-aged. Instead we plan to live in some eternal now which will lead on to something better, something more complete than what we had before. This movement from present to future is a sequence that can hardly be orchestrated. Instead it has to be lived. Cultivating simplicity, we confront the mystery of how things happen, of actual occasions, droplets of time and experience flowing past the sides of the ship as we knife forward into dark seas, seas without a map. We stand at the bow and feel the lurch and the swell. The sea is in our faces. We move, not knowing how, from one zone to the next.

Sometime in our spiritual travels, as a complete surprise, we notice it has become winter. The waves crashing over the deck are icy cold and gray. For the first time we know we are not going to become old; we are, without perhaps fully admitting it, already old. Youth and middle age are behind us. This change has occurred, it seems, without preparation, without fair warning.

My friend John Chase was a humorist. "The reason why I'm not doing so well at being old," he said in his eightieth year, "is that I don't have any practice."

But haven't we been preparing all along? Haven't our lives up to now given us some kind of practice?

Loving Old People

The people I first loved were old. Their faces were creased and lined, crisscrossed by cobwebs of experience. Even so, they were mostly merry. My grandmother's eyes were brown; her style was mischievous. My great aunt, my grandmother's younger sister, who was almost as close to me, had eyes of china blue. Gray-haired when I first knew them, they gradually went white. A dignity, there from the first, grew sharper and more definite. What I remember most about them, however, was laughter.

So in the daily round of childhood, the routines of mornings and evenings, my grandmother Lucy and her sister Eula became my evening stars, my bright example of being old at its best. I thought they were old. In fact, they were women in their early sixties then. They were able-bodied, energetic, vigorous. Yet they were people of a time gone by. They could remember how things had been once, in some former era I longed to hear about. They were charmers, spellbinders, storytellers. I loved to hear them talk, and their talk was always intermingled with a kind of prayer. They were the ones who taught me to pray, intertwining prayer and storytelling at bedtime, in a way so enjoyable I hardly ever wanted it to end. But more than that, they taught me prayer by example. Each morning they devoted time to Bible reading; at any time in their conversation, it seemed, a Bible saying could slip naturally in.

My mother went out to work. Along with my father, she was one of the breadwinners. My grandmother Lucy, whom I called Nui, was my primary caretaker for that reason, the one who was there when I fell or scraped myself or got in trouble somehow. A great intimacy came about because she was always there. Eula, who lived just a few blocks away, taught me to read when I was too young for school. Eula was a schoolteacher who believed in early reading. She herself had learned to read at age four, bored because her older sisters and brother were at school. While her mother did the mending and handwork, Eula sat nearby, coaxing her mother to teach her the alphabet, and scrawling the letters with a piece of slate. She was determined! Because Eula opened the world of reading to me, and the world of spiritual life, she became a lifelong friend.

What literary people they were! I remember how much both Nui and Eula loved nursery rhymes and loved to read them with me. It was part of the Englishness of my growing up. Admittedly, we had been Americans for many generations. (My first American ancestor, John Ogden, had come from England in 1640.) But in some ways my family retained an English sensibility, a link with the past, with generations of people handing things down: thimbles, traditions, family stories, customs, loyalties, ideals. I remember sitting next to Eula on her upstairs porch, flooded with love and sunshine. She taught me how verses galumphed; she made it exciting to read. I remember vivid moments: wicker porch chairs with chintz-covered cushions, frosty glasses of root beer, a china sugar bowl shaped like a pig, Dick and Jane seeing Spot run. I remember straining to form words in my mind; I remember breakthroughs, light dawning. Many years later I saw it all happen again, when my own children learned to read, their small faces bending close to the page, frowning to work out words from baffling letter squiggles. Most of all I remember the triumph, the joy: Eula's, my children's, my own. Learning to read set us loose on an adventure of mind and heart.

Still another white-haired figure was my cousin Lalita Tenney. Lalita was a nurse. And she was exotic, foreign, having been born in Belize. Lalita spoke English with a Spanish accent. Around her cheerful face was an aureole of white hair under her starched white nurse's cap. When I grew old, I wanted to look just like her. I am told she took care of me when I was an infant, in Touro Hospital, New Orleans, where I was born. I don't remember that. What I do remember is that she nursed me through pneumonia when I was hospitalized at age nine.

I remember clouds of moisture on the plastic walls of my oxygen tent, sealing me away from the world. I remember the fear. I remember taking penicillin (an experimental drug in those days) around the clock. Also I remember Lalita's golden smile breaking over me like morning.

So began my fascination with older people; and the fascination grew. I spent many hours with my older relatives: long enough to notice that old men colored their hair with funny-looking tints; long enough to notice the tight, artificial blue-gray curls that old women wore home from the beauty parlor; long enough to notice the eccentricities of the old, little lapses of memory ("Now, where did I put my glasses?" "Wasn't my shopping list right on this table?" "Let me see, what was it I came in here for?").

Perhaps not every child is so surrounded with grandmothering and grandfathering figures. (Among the grandfathering figures, I have a sudden vivid picture of my paternal grandfather, E. G., dapper in his straw hat, three-piece suit and hightop shoes; and Eula's husband, Oscar, a university economics professor, generally at work among his books or deep into the newspaper.)

LOVING OLD PLACES

I was an only child, bookish, thought to be gifted, often lonely. I learned to amuse myself with crayons and paper, with modeling clay and blocks, with books most of all. I loved old places and the formality of the past. Often, because my mother worked and was, for much of my childhood, a single parent, she took me with her to places where she was on assignment. In this way I became the one child most in attendance at meetings of the Louisiana Historical Society, where almost everyone was old.

The meetings were held at the Cabildo, one of the historic government buildings of New Orleans, beside the St. Louis Cathedral, near Jackson Square. In the Sala Capitular, where the society often met, the Louisiana Purchase had been signed. In an adjoining room was a death mask of Napoleon, and the walls were lined with portraits of the early Spanish governors of Louisiana.

To me, the building and the society's members both seemed ancient. The Cabildo's staircase, with its wide steps, was sinking into the soft Louisiana earth. The structure seemed none too secure, it smelled of mildew and the past. Child of the imagination that I was, I loved it all. In this place I could walk into some bygone time. Raised in the English tradition, I was drawn by the French and Spanish past, dazzled by flags hanging high in the old cathedral. Here it was possible, like children in storybooks, to travel back in time.

So, in this way I came to cherish old age. To me, older people were bearers of a colorful past, heirs to the customs of another time. Mrs. Henry Landry de Freneuse I remember as my earliest example of what it was to be Creole. I remember her in formal black dresses, wearing a lace mantilla, a fringed Spanish shawl, pearl-decorated combs, using a fan. Later, when I discovered Jean Giraudoux's play "The Madwoman of Chaillot" I knew that I had met his madwoman and her cohorts before. It was at the Louisiana Historical Society.

Perhaps the most glamorous event of all was the gala banquet held on the evening of January 8 each year at Antoine's Restaurant to celebrate the American victory at the Battle of New Orleans in 1815. In those days few children attended this formal affair; I was one of them. It was hard to stay awake through the long-winded formal speeches with their endless repetition of the well-known facts about the Battle. But I loved the ceremony, the formal dress with decorations, the Spanish and French national anthems played by string ensembles. I felt that I was at the center of an ancient, noble and cosmopolitan culture. Everyone there, except my mother and me and one or two others, was honorably, visibly old. So in my storybook way I fell in love with old age, in the same way that I seem to fall for lost causes and forgotten heroines.

SECRETS TO TELL

The old have secrets to tell us, if we only could learn to listen. Children and the old have something in common. God is very fond of them! The Bible leads us to believe that God protects and loves those who are most vulnerable, showering special gifts on them. Children and the very old are in cahoots. They are in possession of secret codes to the meaning of existence. That is why (no doubt you have noticed) they get on very well.

When I was nineteen I played an old lady on the stage. I was Mrs. Hardcastle in a college production of Oliver Goldsmith's eighteenth-century comedy *She Stoops to Conquer*. I loved acting, but more than that I loved becoming old in my imagination. I moved easily into Mrs. Hardcastle's vanity, her gossipy ways, her badgering, her ridiculous flirtations. I learned how to punctuate her funniest remarks with a flutter of her outrageously large fan; I learned how to settle onto a bench with arthritic discomfort and ill ease. Mere slip of a girl that I was, I enjoyed becoming old.

I remember being made up for the role and seeing the lines traced onto my face by an expert makeup artist. He explained to me as he did so where the shadows should fall and how the muscles of the face would change as they grew old. I smiled at him while he educated me.

However much we flirt with it, teasing and pretending our way through such a life change, we do not in reality want to be old. Yet our future is calling to us. I remember thinking (when the time came) what a grand old lady I would be; I coveted the beauty of old age; what I wanted was the peace, the charm, the wisdom, the surrender that certain old people seemed to possess.

We know our future is calling. Our future is to be old. Every day leads us relentlessly into the unknown. We are moving on uncharted seas. As believers, we think our faith should strengthen us for the voyage. But does it? Does faith make things as easy as all that? Are we sure that we really approve of the way God has arranged things? Do we really care for the plan? Do we wish the Lord had consulted us beforehand, or given us some way to compromise? We are afraid that they will come for us as they did for Peter and lead us where we do not want to go.

Yet in the faces of the gracious old, a kind transparency attracts us and leads us on. In the loving faces of the old who are at peace with themselves and what they have done, who live each day drenched in grace, we see the possibility of our own transformation, of what we may become. We long to be not only old but good and old, with the cup of long life, life well lived, running over and falling into our laps. How will we find this rare grace, this beauty of many days?

SPIRITUAL EXERCISE

At some point in the aging process, we are startled to realize that we have moved into the latter phase of the journey. The first thing we may do to cushion the blow is to examine our own pictures of old age. Who in our past or present exemplifies old age for us? At what point in life do the later years begin? Make a list of the people who formed your notion of old age. Name them. Then sketch, mentally at least and in writing if possible, what characteristics they had. This is the beginning of your own journey to deal with the question of getting older. Up to now, you have considered them the older folks, the elders. Now you are going to join their ranks, to become one of them. How does that make you feel? Can you accept this idea?

QUESTIONS FOR REFLECTION

- How have you formed your view of getting older?

- When you were young, were certain old people interesting or attractive to you?

- Have you seen older people shunted aside, not valued? In what ways?

- When have you thought of yourself as growing older?

- Is there an "up" side to this business of growing older? Are older people different? Do they seem to have some advantages over those who are younger? Why or why not?

- How does Christian faith enter into your reflections on getting older?

2

GOOD SAILORS

How Earlier Generations May Inspire Us

It was odd, I thought, that when I first came to reflect on getting older, I seized upon the metaphor of a voyage. Why was that?

Of course, "the journey" is the usual metaphor for the spiritual life. Maybe it isn't precisely a biblical phrase. Jesus doesn't speak, as we do, about the journey of faith. But there are journeys throughout the Bible, like the journey of the Israelites in the desert. Possibly the most significant is Abraham's journey of faith. Abraham set out on his journey, following God's command. But no, Abraham's journey was on foot, by caravan. It was not a voyage.

And yet for me the journey of faith—and the journey into maturity—was best expressed by the metaphor of a voyage.

I think I can guess why.

I was turning sixteen when I took my first sea voyage—a cruise out of New Orleans on one of the United Fruit Company steamships (there were at least six of them) called the

Great White Fleet. It was one of the precious times when my mother and I sailed away together on a great adventure into the unknown.

That brief voyage—it was probably a journey of eight days, in the summer of 1952—remains in my mind as a real life passage, a coming of age. My mother, who was always an inspiring figure to me, had thought of a way for us to be together, without distractions, at a time when I was moving out of childhood into maturity. No doubt any vacation would have done as well. But for me the sea voyage had high romantic overtones, making me think of Greek myths and Homer's *Odyssey*.

My mother and I had always been close. Partly that was because my parents had been divorced and my mother was raising me as a single parent (in a day when such arrangements were less usual). Throughout my young life I knew that my mother was different from others: mothers who wore aprons, baked cookies, were homemakers, spent time volunteering. My mother had always worked for a living. But she was not a secretary or a clerk, no. She had founded her own company and established a career. She was one of the first stenotype court reporters in New Orleans, one of the first to establish her own freelance firm.

She had established her firm in 1942 and had reported some of the great wartime proceedings in New Orleans, including meetings of the Joint Chiefs of Staff. I am told she cut quite a figure in the courtroom and was known for her stylish dresses and her modish hats. But more than her looks, my mother had a presence. Because she had a keen ear for the spoken word, she could capture a longshoreman's testimony as easily as the words spoken by a captain or ship owner on the witness stand. She loved the adventure of all courtroom proceedings, but often I felt that her first love was maritime work. For her the Mississippi River and the Port of New Orleans had a certain glamour. She put the New Orleans admiralty lawyers on a pedestal and taught me to feel the same. In the mid-1950s she was the reporter for a number of congressional committees, and though I knew little of what she actually did (she was often under oath about some proceedings) I enjoyed the stories she told about courtroom drama and humor. All this achievement by age forty! She spoke with authority; yet she still had youthful enthusiasm. Her presence was more than just stylish dressing. She was intelligent, intellectually curious, thoughtful and had a crackling sense of humor. To me, my mother was someone to admire and to follow. I wanted to be what she was. And I wanted to justify her faith in me.

A MOTHER'S INFLUENCE

A mother's influence can be enormous. She represents security and stability, a foundation, a link to tradition. C. S. Lewis, whose mother died when he was nine, expressed that loss in his autobiography, *Surprised by Joy.* "With my mother's death," Lewis wrote, "all settled happiness, all that was tranquil and reliable, disappeared from my life. There was to be much fun, many pleasures, many stabs of joy; but no more of the old security. It was sea and islands now; the great continent had sunk like Atlantis." (Notice the ocean-going metaphors!) Lewis was the younger of two boys, and both were homeschooled by the mother. No question, his love of stories and literature were gifts from his mother's teaching. And both his parents had loved books.

Lewis captures his memory of this childhood world. "I am a product of long corridors, empty sunlit rooms, upstairs indoor silences, attics explored in solitude, noises of gurgling cisterns and pipes, and the noise of wind under the tiles. Also, of endless books."

This book-loving environment had also been part of my childhood, though I can lay no claim to long corridors or the noise of wind under the tiles. The houses were small, but the depth of vision was great. My mother taught me to love Wordsworth when I was very young, and I was soon able to quote snatches from his wonderful poems.

And this prayer I make
Knowing that nature never did betray the heart that
    loved her;
'Tis her privilege, through all the years of this our life
To lead from joy to joy.

No doubt that the first way I was shaped by my mother was through a love not only of poetry but of language. Keep in mind that Wordsworth was the most influential English poet of my mother's day (with Coleridge a close second). By the time I was in high school and college, this influence remained strong. Perhaps it was beginning to fade, but I didn't know it, for my mother and all of my English teachers had been formed in Wordsworth's school.

Reflecting on my mother's influence, I see that she was my first and most influential teacher, not only in matters of English poetry but in the entire project of how to live, the school of life.

What were the things she taught me? Often they were life lessons learned from her by observation. I saw her moving forward into the future and I thought, *That is how to do it; that is the way it should be done.* She showed me the value, let's say, of innovation and risk-taking without lecturing me about it.

Sometimes she talked about principles of ethics and fair play. Good work, an honorable day's work, living up to the highest standards, taking one's talents seriously and giving the best one could—these were her values, and she lived them. I watched her do it. But I didn't realize she was also living out values she couldn't fully articulate: how to take a risk, how to lean your weight into something you believed in, long before you could possibly know for sure how it might work out.

A VISIONARY ATTITUDE

Born in 1912, my mother transcended the limitations placed on women in her time. And she did it without a trace of feminist rage or noisy rhetoric. In her generation the main question raised about women in the business world often had something to do with Rosalind Russell's padded shoulders and the notion that women would lose their femininity if they had to compete with men. Perhaps that was why my mother developed a stylish and charming femininity, not just in her attire but in her manner. Her style was never flirtatious or exaggerated. No, it was both charming and confident. She never attempted to dominate situations. Instead, she was collaborative and easy to know.

But at the same time she did not accept the limitations on women in her youth.

She had attended both college and secretarial school in a time when a woman was expected to work as a secretary, a typist, a stenographer or a clerk. When she decided to study court reporting, she was taking a chance. Even if she developed the skill, would she be able to find employment? The top free-lance court reporters in New Orleans were men, and they wrote shorthand. My mother studied the stenotype machine, and the machine itself was a novelty, an innovation. The new technology seemed to suggest that times were changing. Partly, the news value carried her forward. Mastering the new way of writing shorthand, by machine, gave her something of a way in. But she was able to envision a future in which she would have her own company, her own clients. As a small child I watched her practicing the stenotype machine, watched the stenotype paper folding into a column, watched her pause to read back what had just been said. She was diligent. She was determined. And she was entrepreneurial, willing to take a risk, to form her own company in a time when many thought (and said) it couldn't be done.

Without knowing it I was learning something about a life calling, about a sense of vocation. My mother was a strongly traditional person, from a family of long-standing in Louisiana. But no one in the family in those days (the 1930s) had any kind of established organization or even a whiff of success. My mother's family was sustained by a sense of gentility, good values and Christian faith. Certainly there was a strong sense of character in the generations that shaped her. Part of our family lore was the way her grandparents had dealt with financial loss, their family home and plantation "sold out from under them" because the taxes had not been paid. This family story, by the time I came along, had grown into the status of a myth, a challenging narrative of how to exercise courage in times of hardship and loss.

But she did not dwell on the past (even though she loved the family stories and admired what her grandparents stood for) but focused on the future. Obviously she took stock of her own talents, her love of words and language. She went to college (the first woman in her family to gain a college degree). She trained in social work. She tried practice teaching. She went to secretarial school. Gradually, she gained a vision of what she was good at, where her talents might lead. She could see only part way into the future. But she took a chance on a kind of work and life that had to be imagined. She walked toward a future she could only partly see.

I wanted to be just like her.

LEADERSHIP AND INNOVATION

When my mother founded her second company (by now it was the 1960s), I could follow step by step the process of innovation and leadership that guided her. No longer a child, I myself was in the New York business world when my mother began to inch into founding another company, without letting go of active participation in the first one.

Where had the vision come from? Now, for the first time I saw how my mother dreamed up a business idea, the intersection between her own talents, the need and opportunity as she saw it, the possible benefit to the community as well as to herself. For her, business life was intermingled with creative insight and love of the community. She loved New Orleans. It was more than just the place where she lived. It was a rich culture out of which so much creative beauty had come: music, celebration, parades, the intermingling of cultures, Mardi Gras, showmanship, masquerade. For her, New Orleans was a vision of possibilities. In founding a new tourism company, she dreamed of sharing more completely the culture that had meant so much to her.

In fact, she probably did not know at first that she was starting something new. As a court reporter, her company was at the fringes of conventions visiting New Orleans, meetings in which some important talk had to be taken down and transcribed. New Orleans itself was changing to attract the convention trade. Civic leaders approached her to suggest that a new kind of enterprise might be needed, one for which she was well qualified. Some were concerned that conventions visiting New Orleans were not getting a favorable impression of the city. Someone with business savvy, someone who really appreciated New Orleans, could provide a new kind of service. The term *hospitality industry* was a brand new idea. Would my mother be willing to get involved? Could she help organize out-of-hotel services and spouse programs? At first it didn't seem so different from the court-reporting work (and convention-reporting work) that she was already doing. But soon, she realized that she had entered a brand new territory.

By 1965 she had hired two younger employees who shared the vision she was beginning to develop. They too had a cultural attachment to New Orleans and to the idea of showing conventioneers more than just Bourbon Street. Before long her new company became one of the first four destination-management firms in the United States, the first in New Orleans. Later on dozens would be formed to capture the tourism boom and profitability of the Crescent City.

My mother's third venture came into being ten years later. In the mid-1970s she noticed how many book projects were coming her way. Some of them were books that she could represent by starting a literary agency. Others were manuscripts that could be shaped into books and published on a small scale for local and particular audiences. By then, she looked for my husband's expertise and collaboration. He was an editor in a New York publishing house and knew many of the New Orleans authors who might become her clients. He thought her third company was a good idea.

By the time I went to work for my mother, in 1980, she was sixty-eight and running three companies that she had founded. The court reporting firm, though still a sole proprietorship, was called Dietrich and Bendix (David Bendix having joined the firm with a major court reporting reputation and clientele); the tourism firm was Helen R. Dietrich, Inc., but often did business as Dietrich Tours and Entertainment; and the literary enterprise was the Habersham Corporation, with its literary agency doing business under the trademarked name Southern Writers.

By now, my mother's tourism firm was widely known and was driven by a strong sales and marketing effort. Helen R. Dietrich, Inc., was soliciting conventions throughout the United States and gaining notice through a multimedia show that show-cased the delights of New Orleans and positioned my mother as the doyenne of New Orleans tourism. While I was still living in New York City in 1979, I was invited to a showing of this multimedia presentation on Dietrich's work. There on the screen was my mother, sitting in a New Orleans patio and talking about the special events her company could arrange for conven-tion visitors and VIPs. As the show ended, a man sitting one row ahead of me turned to his associate and said, "You know, I have actually met Mrs. Dietrich. She is remarkable."

I had worked for more than a decade on Madison Avenue, and I knew the power of the media. Now I saw it in evidence in a small-scale (but very targeted) multimedia show about my mother's tourism company. Everyone in the room was a repre-sentative of a major corporation or trade organization planning to meet in New Orleans and wanting to determine which destination-management firm they should hire. The same prin-ciples that worked for selling soap and detergent were in evi-

dence here, and I understood the salesmanship through and
through. But one element was a complete surprise to me, not
part of the selling package I was used to. This time the product
was not a bar of soap or a brand of detergent. No, it was my
mother herself, her love of New Orleans, her appreciation of
hospitality and entertainment. Her firm had gained the reputation of being the best destination-management firm in New
Orleans. And the city itself was seen as a major destination. All
at once I understood that my mother was becoming a legend. I
stood in the Four Seasons restaurant on Park Avenue (where the
multimedia show had been screened) and pinched myself. Is this
really me? Is it really us? Or just the magic of multimedia?

Yet on some level I understood how authentic and what a
major life achievement it was. I had always perceived my mother
as a bright light, a legendary person, someone with star quality.
And she had worked so hard, with such insight and determination. Moreover she had chosen well—the thing she believed in,
the thing she loved to do. On another level I knew she had
done these things not only for herself but for us, to provide for
both my grandmother and me, to establish stability in her life
and ours.

For years I had been consulting with my mother's firm, helping them to write proposals and brochures, showcasing their
particular selling story. That year they wanted a new slogan,
and the words came easily to mind: "The Dietrich dazzle is
unmistakable."

How Faith Enters In

I also learned about faith from being my mother's companion
on the journey. She rarely talked about faith, but she lived it.
She had trusted in God and had sailed into uncharted waters,

navigating the life journey with a strong sense of God's providential care.

My family was religiously divided. That is to say, while we were all Christians, we could not seem to agree about denominations. My paternal grandmother was Lutheran, passionately so; her husband a lapsed Roman Catholic. On my mother's side most were Episcopalians. A few turned to Christian Science. Some were churchgoers, some stayed at home and did their gardening or correspondence on Sundays.

My mother's faith in God's providential care was buttressed by her spiritual friendship with my grandmother. Together they prayed and read the Bible through many a business crisis. They prayed for business problems to be solved, for sickness to be cured, for angry competitiveness in the office to give way to harmony and understanding. Together they relied on God and prayed for his intervention in the muddle of business affairs. They prayed for checks to arrive and for payrolls to be met. There was a simplicity, a childlike confidence to their reliance on God, sustained by particular verses from Scripture. I too was shaped by their deep reliance on prayer and God's providential, intervening care. Also they showed me an example of how a daughter's faith may be shaped by her mother's. My mother consulted my grandmother about many business decisions. She relied on her wisdom and was nourished by her example of faith.

Each of them navigated the later years with confidence in God and a cheerful reliance on him. Whatever the temptation to anxiety, they maintained a positive attitude. "Do not worry about anything, but in everything by prayer and supplication with thanksgiving, let your requests be made known to God. And the peace of God, which surpasses all understanding, will guard your hearts and your minds in Christ Jesus" (Philippians 4:6-7 NRSV). My mother had, besides the Bible verses, other wisdom sayings that sustained her, and some of them had a seagoing, salty flavor: "No mariner ever distinguished himself upon a smooth sea."

So, as I reflected on the life journey, I saw the need for adaptation, for a change of course when obstacles loomed up suddenly on the way. The voyage metaphor was apt, even if it wasn't drawn from Scripture. In my imagination Greek and Roman literature also had a part to play. As in Homer's *Odyssey* and Vergil's *Aeneid*, our own journeys are rarely smooth sailing. Siren songs may distract us. There are monsters in the deep. Sometimes dangers lurk on uncharted seas. But I thought there was wisdom in what Aeneas said to his sailors when disaster struck. Yes, they had been shipwrecked. But he wanted them to be grateful for their survival and move on. "Perhaps one day," he said to them, "it will be a pleasure to remember even these things."

Now that was a positive attitude.

SPIRITUAL EXERCISE

In a relationship with an older relative or friend, one whose life is reaching its term, celebrate and rejoice in the achievements and pleasures of what has happened up to now. I was fortunate to have an early warning of my mother's declining health, one that permitted me to organize a celebration of her long, fifty-year entrepreneurial career. I will always be grateful to God for the opportunity to do this—at an elegant event sponsored by the New Orleans Board of Trade. A less elaborate event, however, would have accomplished the same aim: to celebrate, gratefully, a gifted life and a generous giver.

QUESTIONS FOR REFLECTION

- Who in your life has encouraged and defined you? Give an example or tell a story about how this person influenced you. Even if you can't narrow it down to one person, can you name several mentors who helped to shape your life, including your spiritual formation?

- What have you learned by observation of others rather than by focused teaching or discussion? What special values did you learn?

THE FAR HORIZON

Let Not Your Heart Be Troubled

All around me, for decades it seems, I have heard people speak about the ways they are planning and preparing for the later years.

First of all, there is financial planning. Wise individuals are putting money aside, working with financial planners to help it earn interest and grow.

Then there is the question of retirement. Some of us have worked long years for a single organization and have developed a retirement package. The main quandary seems to be not whether to retire but when, and what to do afterward.

Another question that arises is where to live. Houses that were once just the right size when our children were at home now seem impossibly large. And then, if we own a home, we constantly have to maintain it, to worry about the roof, the painting, the plumbing, the necessary repairs. One way to navigate the later years is to simplify our living arrangements, moving to smaller quarters, getting a lower rental or mortgage payment. Downsizing our obligations is one way to have, we hope, a greater freedom. Sometimes the move is also to a new community, to be closer to a married son or daughter, closer to grandchildren. Along with downsizing our obligations comes downsizing our possessions, which can become an occupation in itself.

All these practicalities make sense. These are some ways we plan for the future, meaning to be frugal and practical. We want to build a hedge against uncertainties. But to navigate the later years requires much more than financial planning, real estate decisions or possible relocation. In the later years we enter more deeply into the present; at the same time we stretch into the future. Mainly, the questions we deal with are spiritual questions. The matters we are dealing with are spiritual.

What will we do with our lives? What new challenges lie ahead? How will we become fully the people we are meant to be?

The later years should be years of spiritual growth and maturity. "Even though our outer nature is wasting away," Paul writes to the Corinthians, "our inner nature is being renewed day by day" (2 Corinthians 4:16 NRSV). Paul here is speaking to a disciplined community of practicing Christians. He is speaking of the renewal that happens in our ongoing relationship to God in Jesus Christ.

WHAT I WAS MEANT TO BE AND DO

In the later years we pause to reflect on how we will remain active, how we will be refreshed and renewed. We are reaching to complete our lives, to be what God has destined us to be. We ask ourselves fundamental questions. *What was it I was created for? What have I done with my life so far? How shall I spend the remaining time?*

The word *vocation* comes to mind. When I was young the word had a narrow meaning, especially among Catholics, of those who were called to serve God in religious life. In the secular world the word had come to mean a particular kind of work or training. There were vocational schools in which one could learn a trade. Very often these vocational schools were concentrating on nonintellectual kinds of work, leaving to the colleges and universities the possibility of professional training.

But everyone, I think, is called. Everyone has a life vocation. We see it most readily in people who have made some major contribution to the world. Einstein's calling was scientific theory. Dante and Milton were called to be poets.

Consider this famous prayer by John Henry Newman:

God has created me
To do Him some definite service;
He has given some work to me
Which He has not committed to another.

I really believe this is true. It is part of the uniqueness of each person. Early in life, even in childhood, we discover the things we love to do, the things we excel in. For some it is the joy of physical expression, playing a sport, running, doing gymnastics, dancing. For others it is the talent of making and building things, woodworking, carpentry, refurbishing and painting, redecorating houses and repairing them, becoming a mechanic who understands cars. Some are good at electronics, a huge category that has made a profound contribution to modern life. Some simply excel at communications, and they find ways to develop this gift, by teaching, speaking, acting and directing, writing and performing and in countless other ways. And we do these things not only for ourselves but for the sake of others: to please others, to give ourselves to them, to help them, to enhance their lives.

When we come to the later years, we are still exploring and pursuing this life calling. Possibly we are making an abrupt shift from paid work to unpaid work, volunteering to serve on boards and develop community activities. Perhaps we are offering the skills we developed in the business world to nonprofit organizations, church committees and boards. Sometimes we turn to study groups with our peers to explore the books we now have leisure to read. Some of us may develop skills that are both creative and demanding. My friend Louise (a retired mathematics teacher) has taken up quilting, and I know that her quilting work is satisfying, disciplined and creative. No doubt, in some way that I can't comprehend, it is also mathematical.

In Newman's prayer this life vocation is a form of service to God, doing a kind of work he has committed individually to each person. The life calling is a response to an invitation from God, which can be discovered first in our gifts and talents and second in our motivations. What is it that we do that really gives us pleasure, insight and joy? My daughter Sarah is a fine painter in oils, who does landscapes, still lifes and portraits. In my case it is surely writing and speaking. I also think that reading and study are part of my life calling.

THE INCONSOLABLE SECRET

Some teachers of the spiritual life want us to plunge into the immediate moment. But the spiritual life also has a far horizon.

In all seasons of our lives, but especially the later ones, we feel a yearning, a pull to the future, a desire for God which C. S. Lewis speaks of as desire for a "far country."

Lewis mentions the "inconsolable secret" that is in every human heart, the desire for God. This is a desire not merely to know God in our prayer lives but ultimately to be fully in his presence, to meet him. In the past our religious ancestors voiced this in hymns. Some of these took their metaphors from the book of Revelation:

Shall we gather at the river,
Where bright angel feet have trod,
Shall we gather at the river
That flows by the throne of God.

Of course, all these longings are buried deep. One of the reasons why church worship is so appealing is that it allows us to voice these longings in hymns and Scripture without the embarrassment of admitting them to another living soul.

The words of many liturgical services are addressed to God the Father in his full glory and desirability:

Through all eternity you live in unapproachable light. . . .
Countless hosts of angels stand before you to do your will.

But the truth is, there are multiple images of God embedded in our Scripture and worship, and many of them show him as a loving Provider, a protective Father, an intimate Friend.

This yearning for God and this desire to be with him and to please him is with us throughout the life journey. There's plenty of theology to explain all this, much of it under the heading of the divine initiative. God has created us out of love, and he desires us. The power of his love exerts a constant pull to be reunited with him, both now and later, beyond the boundaries of the life we are living now.

THE GIFT OF LIVING WELL

How do we draw nearer to God in the later years? In some sense I think this is related to the question of time. In the later years our time is shorter, we may sense that we have only a certain time left. But in another sense time opens up for us. These latter days are open territory and they seem like pure gift. What will we do with ourselves? How will we respond to the inward yearnings we feel—yearnings to be closer to God, to embrace fully the gift of living well?

Instinctively, I think, we explore the things we love, but in a deeper way. Certain activities put us in touch with a deeper reality, and we intuitively turn to those.

Sometimes we make an easy turn to what is beautiful. My husband and I currently live in a small house, and he keeps it filled with flowers. When the weather permits we sit outside in the garden. My husband insists on cutting the grass himself. Often we go on short drives in the neighborhood, along streets lined by flowering trees, crepe myrtle and Japanese magnolia, or along country roads where the fields stretch out into remarkable landscapes. Sometimes we talk furiously at first. Then our talk slows till we can actually see what is in front of us. We move into the scenes. We appreciate the beauty of the scenes we are passing through.

We do not talk about "the inconsolable secret," the yearning for God and the longing for heaven embedded in our hearts. But we are bathed for a time in the reality of things, and the sky, the clouds, the daylight descending or ascending, the sudden beauty of a cornfield—all these speak to our hearts in ways that are indescribable.

LOVE OF NEIGHBOR

One of the ways we are being transformed is through love. In later life we become more conscious of this. Take the whole question of "loving my neighbor," which is surely a great imperative of the spiritual life. But how do we actually practice this? Sometimes we are baffled by the religious language this command of faith is framed in. It is hard to appropriate this "love of neighbor" for ourselves. What does it mean to love our neighbor? Have we done this all along? Should we aspire to do it more? Or is it just a natural outflow of the converted heart?

Sometimes I get a snapshot of what this love of neighbor may mean and how it is expressed. It seems that love of neighbor is often shown in a spontaneous response to God's grace.

My husband was working as an editor, part of an editorial team, on Billy Graham's autobiography, *Just As I Am*. Because my husband wanted me to meet Dr. Graham, I was invited into some informal situations where he and his associates were present. There was always a concern for privacy and anonymity, so everyone was very close-mouthed about where Dr. Graham would be, and sometimes a cover name was used.

One such occasion was a dinner in a large seaside hotel, where about a dozen people were present. The atmosphere was festive but nonchalant. I knew this much at least: when you are introduced to a famous person, you should interact easily with him or her, not overreacting to the person's importance or fame.

But suddenly the hotel waiter said to Dr. Graham, with astonishment: "I know who you are! I know who you are!"

How did Dr. Graham react to this? He quietly entered into a private conversation with the waiter, which went on for ten minutes at least. They were talking about the Christian life. Billy Graham did not know this man, would probably never see him again and could easily have brushed off his attentions. Instead, he entered into a moment of friendship with him, certainly on pastoral terms but also on terms of equality. It was an exchange of sudden, out-of-the-blue friendship. For me there was an extra fillip. The waiter was Hispanic and spoke with a pronounced accent. He was overjoyed at being in Dr. Graham's presence, but amazed at Dr. Graham's generous response. One might say the waiter completely forgot himself, but then Dr. Graham did too.

As I watched this exchange taking place, I thought it was what Jesus must have done on many occasions when a stranger approached him in faith. He responded generously. This kind of encounter happened so often in Jesus' life that the disciples had to protect him from the crowds.

RANDOM SPIRITUAL CONVERSATIONS

When someone unexpectedly strikes up a spiritual conversation with me, do I consider myself God's messenger? I may bring some good and joy into another person's life.

Not long ago, rather surprisingly, a dental hygienist engaged me in a spiritual conversation. "I'm not very reflective," she said. But obviously some of the great issues of midlife were weighing on her heart. "A classmate of mine is very reflective," she went on. "He sends out an e-mail newsletter every Monday with spiritual questions to ponder." Why, she wondered, wasn't she like that?

I gave her a response about the uniqueness of each person,

the ways we respond to God's grace, the different ways we use our gifts and talents. I praised her for the work she does and the way it benefits her patients. A light broke over her face. "Thank you," she said. "I've been thinking over what I have done with my life."

Then I remembered the story of C. S. Lewis and his barber. Lewis showed up for a haircut unexpectedly, after a trip to London was canceled. And his barber said, "I was praying that you would come today." It was like a scene from the book of Acts, Philip being sent by the angel out on the Gaza Road.

Later in life we are beginning to become wisdom figures in the eyes of those who are younger. When we are approached for advice and counsel we should respond generously. Things like this may happen throughout our lives. However, it seems to me that in later years we may experience them more often and more profoundly. Is this because people instinctively turn to older men and women as advisers and counselors, giving us credit for wisdom because of our years? I think so. Our generous response to such approaches and interruptions is part of our practice of the Christian life.

THE PURSUIT OF FRIENDSHIP

Another important way we practice the Christian life is through our close friendships. Getting older makes us more aware of friendship as a gift from God. Of course, Jesus is our great example of what it is to be a friend. He speaks about friendship in deep ways. "I call you friends," he says to his disciples, "because I have made known to you everything that I have learnt from my Father" (John 15:15). Jesus practices friendship. He gathers friends around him, walks the roads with his companions, breaks bread with them, talks with them. Through Jesus and his friends we see that friendship is life changing.

There is something quite amazing about the friendships of our youth which remain strong over time. By staying in touch with friends of an earlier day, some of them now in far-off places, we are kindling the old fires. At times we must change from one community to another, leaving a circle of friends behind. That is when we realize how precious friendship is. How will we find new friends? How will we start again?

Friendship flowers over and over, springing up in totally surprising ways, often through seeking common goals. We make friends at work or in community service or in groups dedicated to the spiritual life. When we enter into study groups, book discussion groups and committee work, we are opening ourselves up to friendship.

There are many dimensions to a good marriage. Friendship is one of them. In fact, counselors often say that married partners must become friends if they expect to stay married for long.

THE UNPREDICTABILITY OF THINGS

However much we may plan for the later years, we cannot factor in, fully, the unpredictability of things. Investments may fail. A major illness may drain the coffers. Adult children may hit unexpected reversals of fortune and turn to us for help. Even natural disasters may sweep away the houses we built and the dreams we planned on.

That is why faith is the most important resource for the later years. Jesus speaks of the man who built his house on rock and the one who built his house on sand. "Everyone who listens to these words of mine and acts on them will be like a sensible man who built his house on rock. Rain came down, floods rose, gales blew and hurled themselves against that house, and it did not fall: it was founded on rock" (Matthew 7:24-25).

Of course, we must be prudent and plan as effectively as we can. But the best thing we can build for the future is the structure of our faith. God is the rock and represents our only real security in a changing world.

READING WITH CHARLES DAVIS

I was shocked to learn that our friend Charles Davis, a major medieval historian and Dante scholar, had lost his eyesight in a hospital accident. I consulted a mutual friend, who told me that Charles would welcome a visit from me.

When I went to see Charles in his office at Tulane University, I found him adjusting well to his blindness. Surrounded by books on three walls of his spacious office, he was also equipped with the latest in technology: computers that talked to him so that he could continue his work. He was still teaching (with the help of graduate assistants, who escorted him to class) and still publishing (with the assistance of his grown sons, who helped him to complete scholarly articles). Still, Charles told me, there was a certain gap. He had no one to read Latin with him.

It was one of the most haunting requests I had ever heard. I understood that Charles knew my facility in Latin. In my undergraduate days he had given me his own Oxford University copy of Vergil. In those days, when he was a young faculty member at Tulane, I had found him dazzling because he had a D.Phil. from Oxford (St. John's College) and his dissertation had been published by the Clarendon Press. Now, so many years later, Charles was at the pinnacle of a distinguished career. Also he was blind, and it was time for me to reciprocate his kindness. I volunteered to read Latin with him.

Once a week I spent an hour, sometimes longer, in Charles's office. We began by reading book VI of the *Aeneid*, in which Aeneas descends to the underworld. Charles especially requested that reading because it pertained to a lecture he was soon to give about Dante. I was amazed at his ability to translate from the Latin when the text was read aloud to him. He didn't want to rely, entirely, on my translation skills, but to do some of the work himself.

Sometimes we added readings of Dante into the sessions. Since my Italian was imperfect, we relied on tape recordings by another Dante scholar, and I read the English aloud. Once in a while we read long passages from Milton's *Paradise Lost*. Charles loved Milton but also liked to remind me that he thought Milton inferior to Dante. I only half-believed him and was deeply moved when Charles was able to recite Milton's sonnet on his blindness entirely from memory:

When I consider how my light is spent
Ere half my days in this dark world and wide
And that great talent which is death to hide
Lodged with me useless.

This episode nearly brought me to tears.

The business of reading with Charles went on quite a few years. At some point my husband joined in the reading sessions. During Bill's years with the Jesuits he had spoken Latin as well as studying it. Charles preferred Bill's Italianate accent to mine. Also I think he loved the fellowship of having us both on hand. There was lots of joking and reminiscing about Oxford, a place we all loved.

Toward the end of Charles's life we were reading two essays on friendship, one by Aelred of Rievaulx and one by Cicero. Both were in Latin.

"You should do a translation of these essays," Charles said. "A husband and wife collaboration. I'll write the preface," he said. What an amazingly cheerful spirit he had, right to the end. He transcended his infirmity and accepted it with remarkable grace. I think it had something to do with his strong Christian faith and his vivid perception of heaven.

WE ARE BEING TRANSFORMED

Our faith tells us we are being transformed day by day. As Christians, we believe such change is possible. We assent to the grace of this transformation but can't always sense such positive change taking place. In Scripture this change is often linked to the ways we suffer and the afflictions we endure. "So we do not lose heart . . . for this slight momentary affliction is preparing us for an eternal weight of glory, beyond all measure" (2 Corinthians 4:16-17 NRSV). Our faith assures us that we are being changed, if we cooperate with God's grace, into the persons God meant us to be. This promise of transformation isn't confined to the later years. But in the later years, we may notice it more and more.

C. S. Lewis reminds us that this promise of transformation carries with it a great risk. He cautions us against the power of our choices. Every time we make a choice we are becoming better or worse, more like a heavenly creature or a hellish one. So, while we generally think of transformation as a good thing, we must be on our guard against the moral and spiritual power of the decisions we make.

Transformation isn't just a promise for the later years but for the whole of life. Even so, as we come into the later years, we may be more conscious of our need for change, our desire for change. We long for God and we want to become the people he has called us to be. We open ourselves up to the rich possibilities of the Christian life.

Yes, we must live in the present moment, knowing that God will be fully present to us there. But also we set our sights on the far horizon.

SPIRITUAL EXERCISE

Seek out old friends and forgive old enemies.

I was astonished, when I tried to start forgiving my enemies, to realize how many loose ends were trailing in my life. I am still attempting to identify and forgive the persons against whom I have harbored annoyances and resentments. To forgive an old enemy does not necessarily require renewing the friendship on the same terms or failing to learn from past mistakes. But to reencounter and forgive is cleansing and part of a life's possibility of integration and wisdom.

QUESTIONS FOR REFLECTION

- How have you experienced the opening up of time for God in later life?

- Do you agree that spiritual development is an important resource for the later years? Have you observed this God openness in older people you know? Have you experienced it yourself?

- What do you think about the spiritual opportunities that seem to come to us randomly? Have you experienced such "occasions of grace"?

- In what ways does Jesus provide us with a model for spiritual friendship?

4

THE SPIRITUAL LIFE

Strength for the Journey

Spiritual life—prayer and reflection—can help us develop strength for the later years. Not only do we include a variety of spiritual practices in our lives; also we develop a deeper relationship with God, one that is not based on duty but on genuine friendship.

For me, the relationship with God is the chief love story of my life. And it is always an adventure, often a matter of changing course and finding new ways forward, new beginnings. We are shy about speaking of our love of God in such romantic terms. We speak of "the spiritual life" or "the life of prayer." But in fact, the mystical writers are closer to it when they speak of a journey to God, a journey into God or into the heart of Christ.

Do we pray differently as we grow older? For some, growing older is the first call to prayer. In one way getting older is in itself an experience of God, a sharper opportunity for grace.

We are faced with narrowing options. Intensity is heightened as our choices dwindle. We have to undergo a new experience of conversion akin to the religious conversions we have already had. I have reason to accept what Thomas Merton says: we are converted over and over in our lives, and that each such passage is a deeper and more final rending of the self. Now I understand that getting older is another surrender, like the ones before, but having its own special character and its own supply of grace.

G. K. Chesterton says that surrender is a moment of narrowness: "That intensity which seems most narrow because it comes to the point, like a medieval window." In Chesterton's imaginative figure, the person feels "as if he were looking through a leper's window. He is looking through a little crack or crooked hole that seems to grow smaller as he stares at it."

This surrender that Chesterton describes is not the conscious affirmation of a religious choice. Instead it is what comes before that choice, a moment of abandonment, a sensing of our human boundedness and inadequacy that seems to have extension in space and time. William James describes something similar in different language. He sees surrender of the self as the resolution of a crisis in which the person is "living on the ragged edge of his consciousness, pent in to his sin and want and incompleteness, and consequently unconsolable," and unable to accept an ordinary reassurance that all is well.

Don't I find myself again in a situation that is closing in, where thought and resolution are useless, but it helps to relent and give in? I can't charge forward to overcome this; instead I have to give way and be led, intuitively, into a space that squeezes me tight. I am like Augustine in the garden, wanting to make a choice but unable to do so, unable to put the will into play.

I was saying inside myself, "Now, now, let it be now!" and as I spoke the words I was already beginning to go in the direction I wanted to go. I nearly managed it, but I did not quite manage it. Yet I did not slip right back to the beginning; I was a stage above that, and I stood there to regain my breath. And I tried again and I was very nearly there; I was almost touching it and grasping it, and then I was not there, I was not touching it."

Like Augustine, I am hanging in suspense. Like Chesterton, I am in the gap, the abyss "between doing and not doing such a thing." I am in between the person I was and the person I have not yet become.

Something More Is Asked of Us

For Lewis the experience of God is one of dismantling, unbuckling, letting down resistance, ultimately an undoing. "Now I felt . . . that God was out of reach not because of something I could not do but because of something I could not stop doing. If I could only leave off, let go, unmake myself, I could be there." There are dozens of similar accounts of surrender. Life presents a series of journeys into the void, scampers through the abyss.

Surrender is the necessary undoing for such predicaments, and this surrender does not always bring with it lyrical highs and enthusiastic feelings. Some who have gone through such experiences may give testimonies of joy and appreciation, but their accounts seem nontransferable. Each of us must make his or her own surrender in circumstances that seem to be unique. This kind of surrender is unfaith asking for faith, without confidence of deliverance or rescue. The asking is nevertheless a kind of self-giving.

Getting older, then, is giving way to another painful conversion. I like what the theologian Karl Barth says about conversion when he calls it a powerful summons to halt and advance. That, to me, is how it feels: stopped in my tracks by the powerful realization that youth and middle age have been blown away by storms of change. As C. S. Lewis said about his mother's death, "It was sea and islands now; the great continent had sunk like Atlantis."

This alienation is not unbelief. Instead, it takes place within and during a continuing belief that God exists. This aloneness comes because God is not within our power to control; time is not subject to us but to forces, his forces, beyond our grasp. My alienation is greater than the atheist's; for the God I love and have given my life to will not do it my way; he appears to have forgotten me.

The believer in the suspense of surrender sees God as the rich man did, looking across from hell; knowing there is a blessed vision from which he or she is always to be shut out. The alienation of surrender is in knowing that some bliss may exist but is out of our reach; a bliss to which we feel forever not entitled.

Can we look on this insight as a gift? Surrender is the moment when I see clearly (but hopelessly) where I stand before God. This deep intuition of reality is something given, something we ourselves could not bring about.

Like Augustine, Aquinas, Luther, I say: By myself I can do nothing. I surrender, I relent, I undo myself, and grace comes as pure gift.

Our surrender is giving way to death, a helpless descent into baptismal waters, an abandonment to the unknown. (It may sound stark, but that is how Scripture describes it.) This death is entered into for God without a guarantee of God. The view is closing in. Our breathing space is short. Time is running out. This death taken on God's word is what we say conversion is. Our baptism is in the act of self-surrender, not in the waters when they splash.

Sometimes, in the many surrenders of the spiritual life, we remember our first gift of self. Each gift of self is something new, like nothing that went before. The continuing experience of conversion doesn't shout but becomes more quiet and still.

God is waiting for us. He is accepting the gift we make. He has entered into time for us, to show us what time is. Salvation is an event. God is personal. He has left the ninety-nine to find the one.

The Baptized Imagination

In his own story of conversion C. S. Lewis describes the baptizing of his imagination as one stage in his spiritual journey. While reading a novel by George MacDonald in a railway carriage, Lewis found a way to experience the possibility of holiness. "That night," he says, "my imagination was, in a certain sense, baptized. The rest of me, not unnaturally, took longer."

How clear it is that before we can believe in God, we must imagine the sort of God it is possible to know! This reverent imagining helps us to shatter false images: a God who exists but forgot about us, a God who existed for unlettered folk but not for intellectuals, a God who might exist for philosophy or mathematics but couldn't be reached by phone, a hard taskmaster, unforgiving judge, life force and so on. Out of our own memories we retrieve (so as to deal with them) angers and grievances. From those relived experiences of God we begin to picture him in sharper focus. Now we can permit God to ap-

proach us; we can accept an intimate friendship with him. For
some what is needed is not approachability but transcendence.
Imagination frees us to find the end of our searching, the Lord
our hearts are yearning for. Through imaginative freedom we
may glimpse God as a blazing sun of justice, a Yahweh who
stoops down to lift up the infant, a generous Creator who
knows how to give good things to his children, or the protective Lord we knew in our childhood lullaby.

My own sense of prayer is that the most critical moment is
beginning, but prayer has no necessary sequence. Instead,
prayer is a jewel with many facets. Beginning is not only first
but last, and in between as well. As John Henry Newman says,
"we are ever but beginning." In his sermon "Christian Repentance" we read, "The most perfect Christian is to himself but
a beginner, a penitent prodigal, who has squandered God's
gifts, and comes to him to be tried over again, not as a son but
as a hired servant."

But the point is to begin, and to capture prayer almost as
Audubon might have, in its wilderness setting, on the wing.
The seven facets as I see them are beginning, yielding, darkness, transparency, fear of heights (fear of advancing in the
spiritual life), hoops of steel (spiritual friendship, fellowship and
community), and clinging, an expression—both biblical and
theological—for what used to be called (by some is still called)
unitive prayer.

How is it, everyone wants to know, that experiences of such
depth can happen in our midst, even in middle-class humdrum
lives? The answer is biblical, that God is no respecter of persons,
not class conscious, and shows no partiality. He distributes his
riches even to members of the middle class, once they have laid
down their hostile defenses and surrendered to his will.

LETTING DOWN DEFENSES

Does the Lord actually speak to us in a language we can recognize? Does he speak as he used to in the desert with Moses and our ancestors? We learn how God communicates only after we take some chances. When we squash the reluctances that say, "I don't have time to pray," "God talks to other people, not to me," "I don't know what you're talking about, nothing happens when I pray," or even, "I'm so busy serving the Lord, I don't have time to pray," when we set all these unconvincing excuses aside, that is when actual dialogue can begin.

When we start to drop defenses, we learn (or relearn) that breakdowns in prayer stem less from lack of time, hardly from God's indifference, more likely from some common ailment of ours like fear. Once we know prayer is real, that God is accessible, what often holds us back is reluctance to get involved. We worry that something might be required. Dues will certainly have to be paid. We're afflicted with Peter's fear—we can almost hear ourselves saying, "I never knew the man."

But once we make a surrender of the imagination, other surrenders also may come more easily. Here in the country of the heart, where the Lord can call us by name, we have a sense that almost anything can happen. The table is spread in the wilderness and we are invited to a picnic after all. We know we are sinners, yet we know we are loved. The generous spirit of the Lord is anointing us with forgiveness and acceptance. These are the delights of giving way, with all our faults and feelings, to prayer.

This is no mysticism of the mountaintop. Instead, we are living out our day-to-day existence, traveling back and forth to jobs, to daily errands and chores. There are needy parents asking for more of us, relatives who want more visits, ask for more of our time. How can we give ourselves to prayer with this lot setting up their daily whine? Small trials and annoyances crisscross our days. In this wilderness there is prophetic truth. If we would deny ourselves it is best to do it in the wilderness of every day.

WALKING BY FAITH

Two of the most important aspects of the spiritual life are darkness and transparency. Darkness is an actual experience of confusion and abandonment, of walking by faith without seeing the way. For those who have been raised to think Christian belief is a matter of having all the answers, having a neat-and-tidy worldview with no cobwebs in the corners, the plain fact of darkness may seem something like betrayal, a disappointment or letdown at the very least.

But the truth of prayer is, the more we trust in God, the more he calls us into the mystery of things and wants us to share his own experience of the cross. The surprise is, he lets us do this wherever and whoever we are, as long as we are willing to pray. Such praying does not even have to be fully attentive, disciplined contemplation. We can spend time with God even when not entirely praying—linger on the edge of his consciousness, enjoy him as a companion or presence just over there, somewhere. God isn't always dazzling. Sometimes he is merely friendly. In any event it is our assent that lets him respond to our need.

Alongside this darkness there is transparency: a kind of seeing through the veil, grasping experience more deeply in and through the Lord, because of the Lord. Transparency is a way of describing the effects of prayer without offering guarantees, without referring to specific gifts and blessings like those promised in Isaiah 11 and Galatians 5. Instead of viewing the transforming effects of prayer as attributes of the holy person, it's possible to look out at the world from the viewpoint of the one who prays and find the world more open, more available than before. The person of prayer finds God intensely in "things" and yet is less attached to things. The immediacy of experience makes us speak, as the school of Duns Scotus did, in terms of "thisness," the vision of God in the particular.

By a large shift in our understanding we are plunged into the heart and mystery of things as they are. Who knows where the vision will lead? The call is to come where loving our neighbor might happen without much effort, where forgiveness is not through clenched teeth, but more easygoing. Slowly that stubborn lump of anger or resentment inside of us starts to melt, we sense that we are being healed, we take up our beds and walk.

FRIENDSHIP AS SOUL-GRAPPLING

Perhaps the most striking everyday gift of the Spirit is something I call—borrowing Shakespeare's language—hoops of steel. "Those friends thou hast, and their adoption tried / Grapple them unto thy soul with hoops of steel." This well-documented union of souls is biblical, glimpsed in the love of David and Jonathan, found in the tenderness of Paul and Timothy, mirrored in the intimacy of Augustine and Monica, the passion of Paula and Jerome, the sweet austerity of Benedict and Scholastica. Holiness, it seems, can fuse hearts.

In contemporary life, spiritual direction offers one chance for close spiritual friendship. In prayer groups, such spiritual partnerships come about easily. Spiritual friendship is something that can't be orchestrated or arranged. But it seems to spring up like dandelions wherever people are gathered in Christ's name.

Spirituality is lifelong. And it is usually surprising. Prayer is not always a source of consolation, more often a matter of holding the line, having to keep at it without warm feelings, when memories hurt, things don't go well, resentments escalate. If we look ahead, the way can be forbidding. Yet if we look behind, the complex path shows us how far we have come. We notice how the road twists. We see that we have chosen the Lord again and again, whatever the discipline required, and we see in retrospect that he has not failed us.

There may be things we wanted, things we did not get, rewards that did not come. We must wrestle with haunting memories, disappointments, disenchantments, competitions where we were losers and others won. Even so, we cling to the Lord. We know he cares for us. By faith we hold on.

Gradually, we begin to understand that our prayer has passed far beyond technique, beyond the longing for personal growth, past customary notions of fulfillment. Instead we are clinging less and less to motivational language, and fastening more and more onto the Lord. Prayer is less a matter of petitions, rarely a matter of encounters. We have ceased to wonder whether that figure who met us on the hillside might possibly have been the Lord. Instead there is an intimacy that passes our understanding. We are held in a clasp that is loving and powerful, one that makes demands. Yet we know we have chosen this, our commitment is rooted, radical. There is no slipping loose, no turning back. The path lies straight ahead.

But generalizing about the interior content of prayer is possibly misleading or may raise false expectations. God's way with each one is precisely what is right for each, and nobody ought to wish for someone else's experience. It is tempting, but dangerous, to compare and contrast. Also, to be preoccupied with the glittering extras, voices and visions and such stuff, is something about which spiritual advisers will likely caution us. The so-called fruits of prayer—peacefulness, longanimity, temperance, fortitude and so forth—should also be treated with care. There's a danger in wanting to become accomplished in prayer; a danger in the instinct to show off our prayer experiences for public admiration. Always, we need to be reminded to cling to the Lord and not to the experience—consolation or desolation—of prayer.

GROUPS MAY STRENGTHEN US

In another way, groups are healthy. Highly romantic prayer experiences often have their funny moments. In group sharing, the lighter side of life tends to surface. Burdens become more bearable when shared among members of a group. Community is strengthening. We understand our experiences are authentic. At the same time we see that the point of prayer is to make us more loving and generous. This happens, not all at once, but in good time and unself-consciously as we pray and share our experience in an easy, natural way.

Openness to the needs of others is an almost inevitable consequence. We also develop some real detachment about the things we use and own. Most importantly, we come to want deeper conversion, the next step in the adventure. Together and separately, we are ready for the Lord's call.

A good description of the maturing and stabilizing influence of prayer can be found in the promises of Alcoholics Anonymous. This program of everyday spirituality is based on a practical surrender to the limits imposed by a perilous addiction. It requires complete reliance on God by people who in many instances have not been able to handle the demands and rites of established religion. Clearly, the AA promises celebrate the blessings of Christian prayer. In part they say:

> We are going to know a new freedom and a new happiness. We will not regret the past nor wish to shut the door on it. We will comprehend the word "serenity" and we will know peace. No matter how far down the scale we have gone, we will see how our experience can benefit others. That feeling of uselessness and self-pity will disappear. We will lose interest in selfish things and gain interest in our fellows. Self-seeking will slip away. Our whole attitude and outlook upon life will change. Fear of people and economic insecurity will leave us. We will intuitively know how to handle situations which used to baffle us. We will suddenly realize that God is doing for us what we could not do for ourselves.

Developed in a practical and spiritual program to maintain sobriety, these promises are the fruit of lived experience. AA members experience conversion and live their faith courageously in the context of each day.

We are called both to Christian maturity and to childhood simplicity. All this potentially is ours when we become teachers and examples for one another, when we extend to each other the experience of friendship, commitment and hope.

The journey is ongoing. We yield, naming our experience pilgrimage, growth, maturation, a personal and collective voyage of faith. While both conversion and prayer can be captured in structures and discerned in terms of stages and steps, they are like all love relationships spontaneous, unpredictable, blown by winds of grace.

NOT WHAT WE DO BUT WHAT GOD DOES

The activist mentality of Western culture prompts us to focus repeatedly on the style, the manner, the mechanics, the method of prayer. How should we schedule our devotions? Must we pray in common or alone? Is there a risk that solitary prayer will make hermits out of us? Is it better to pray with or without mental images, with or without words? Should we beseech the Lord or just remain in God's presence? How much time, realistically, should ordinary persons spend in prayer? All these questions are practical, legitimate, worthy of attention, able on the whole to be answered by those who are experienced. Yet to focus on these things too much, too often, may be a distraction from the main point of praying. Our focus should not be on what we do but what the Lord does in us.

In contrast, an activist mentality of another sort measures prayer in terms of its social effects, links prayer to justice and political action. This prayer activism is desirable, legitimate, so long as it doesn't take on a mentality of works righteousness. "By their fruits you shall know them" is now, as always, a proper measure for the depth of spiritual life.

But the more important change is beyond structures, beyond words and images. It is a kingdom of hope that comes to exist in our minds and hearts, a sense of expectation. We are called, we are summoned, we are going somewhere, we are on the road, and the Lord is both at the destination and walking the path with us.

To live the experience of prayer is to enter into a mystery with the Lord. It is the mystery we share when we become childlike and are willing to trust at least a little that things make sense. It is the mystery we share when we visit the sick, welcome the stranger, when we extend ourselves for others. In the growing experience of Christian prayer—private and public, collective and solitary—a good spirit is at work. It is a spirit of repentance. We understand that we are not coming to church to be ministered to but to minister, not to be served but to serve. We take hold of our own salvation, ready to work it out in fear and trembling. The guilt of the past is gone. We learn how to set anxiety aside, and how to be with the Lord in simple ways. Obediently, we render up our work, our skills, our talents, to him and to others for his sake.

THE GRACE OF GETTING OLDER IS SIMPLICITY

"A woman with shorn white hair is standing at the kitchen window," Truman Capote writes in his story *A Christmas Memory*. "She is wearing tennis shoes and a shapeless gray sweater over a summery calico dress." Capote is writing out of the wellsprings of his own memory. This is Sook, his distant cousin, with whom he lived as a small child. There is a deep bond between them, the bond of their parallel vulnerabilities. "She is small and sprightly, like a bantam hen; but, due to a long, youthful illness, her shoulders are pitifully hunched." Her face, Capote remembers, is craggy as Lincoln's, sun-tinted, delicate, finely boned, her eyes sherry-colored and shy. "We are each other's best friend. She calls me Buddy, in memory of a boy who was formerly her best friend. The other Buddy died in the 1880's when she was still a child." But Capote insists that even now, at sixty-something, Sook is still a child. That is the source of the closeness between them.

I recognize my own experience in Capote's story. When I was a child I had such friends: people who were old and, because of their vulnerability, children. Wasn't it also because of their spirituality, their closeness to the Lord, that they were children? They taught me to love God; they taught me how to remain a child always.

When I was twenty-seven I wrote a play in which the best-drawn, perhaps the most sympathetic figure was a woman of eighty. The play concerned a New Orleans Creole family and its tragic determination to found a dynasty. The woman's name was Odile.

"I'm eighty," she says in the first scene. "My face is a cobweb and my hair is spun glass and I take smaller steps than I used to. But I can see clear. I can see far."

When we are young, we think that the old can look directly into the future, into the face of God. As we become older we understand how sometimes God hides his gaze, and as we come closer to the end of our lives we love the things of this life more and more.

Three rain-drenched sparrows in a tree shake themselves loose from the rain. A water-logged hibiscus nods its pink face in our direction. Crepe myrtle trees let their passions run riot through the streets. A splendid sun melts on the river, the silhouette of the city stands against the dawn. Wetness on the windows trembles after the rain. Ivy creeps over the balconies. Babies stir, giggle and fret in people's arms. Books of faded photographs stand open, revealing memories.

I see clearly now that I have to make a deeper commitment to God, offering him not a day, a week, a season, but everything that I am. It is time to work out tough questions, the "unfinished business" in my relationship with God. I understand there are some issues I have been avoiding. These are things I've glossed over, knotty problems I have run away from, hurts I can't handle. Time itself is the issue, more than ever. It is not as though I were asked to clear a space in my calendar; no. It is God's calendar, not mine.

Sometimes I look for refreshment in my spiritual life by a change of place. But more likely what I need is a change of attitude, a difference of the heart. How will I practice simplicity? How will I pour myself out for God and be empty for him?

It is in this time of dwindling choices that we find deepening grace. Viktor Frankl speaks of this when he explores the power of spirituality for the prisoners in Nazi concentration camps. "In spite of all the enforced physical and mental primitiveness of life in a concentration camp," Frankl writes in *Man's Search for Meaning*, "it was possible for spiritual life to deepen. Sensitive people who were used to a rich intellectual life may have suffered much pain (they were often of a delicate constitution) but the damage to their inner selves was less. They were able to retreat from their terrible surroundings into a life of inner riches and spiritual freedom."

OSCAR'S CAMELLIAS: MAKING THE GIFT OF SELF

Even as I celebrate what I have learned about praying as a discipline, about the formal side of spiritual life, I remember those who, for one reason or another, possibly in childhood emotional formation, can't experience religion as I do. For them, God is met in other ways, ways that are not mentioned in terms of faith. An example of this was my great uncle Oscar's magnificent camellia garden.

Can I ever come to terms with the memory of Oscar's camellias? This was my great-uncle's triumph, the crown of a life well-lived. As I reflect on my memories of Oscar, it seems to me that, simply by being closer now to the age he was when I knew him first, I am able to see him more clearly. Is it possible that all my male relatives have been seen through a distorting lens? Did I really know Oscar for the man he was, the dedicated economist and teacher? Now, in a burst of insight I think I know that Oscar's camellias were his spirituality, his worship, his celebration of God's creative power.

The camellia is an exquisite plant that does best in sunny climates, but also can manage with partial shade. Even without their flowers, camellia bushes are handsome. Their leaves are lustrous, broad, ever green. But the flowers are the triumph, appearing, as they do, in winter, as a unexpected blessing, a kind of stunt performed by nature at a time when we least expect it. There are single, semi-double and double forms of camellias, ranging up to as much as four inches across: whites, pinks, red and variegated colors.

When Oscar retired he began to grow camellias. Perhaps he had been growing them all along, but I only began to know about it when I was in college (this would be 1953-1957) when boxes of Oscar's camellias came by post from his home in Lafayette, Louisiana. I remember these flowers now in all their fragility and power: the boxes opened to reveal layers of frail, passionate camellias packed in wet paper, packed with attentiveness and care. They had names; each one was a triumph. We floated them in shallow crystal bowls on side tables, on coffee tables, in the entranceway, in the dining room, of the house on Arabella Street, where the high ceilings and handsome wallpaper, the mahogany staircase and the glass chandeliers sparkled in a kind of retelling of past revels and future celebrations.

It was winter! It is in winter that Louisiana camellias bloom. This too was part of Oscar's triumph, getting his garden to bloom earlier in winter than if nature had taken its course. The gardener must protect his plants from low spots in which cold air settles, from destructive winds, from late, damaging frosts. The scientist as well as the nature lover must bring her skill to bear, planting the camellias where they have the best sheltering by natural or manmade walls, shrubbery and garden fences. To do this properly, the gardener has to understand how wind reacts when it meets a barrier.

If the barrier is a solid fence or wall, the wind jumps up over it like a hurdle, comes down on the other side and keeps going. The only plants protected by the wall are those in the immediate lee. In Louisiana, plants are often covered during frosts; sometimes, if they are planted in tubs, they can be moved indoors. Whatever it takes, it takes skill and attention, energy and commitment, and most of all love.

In my memory now I reconstruct Oscar's loving gift of growing camellias for us. No doubt they were also for himself, his personal celebration of existence. This was the self-gift of his old age, to devote his intellect, his planning, his management talent, his fully lived economics to the beauty of a winter garden, a hymn to the beauty of God.

I Could Leave the World with Today in My Eyes

It is morning. Again, we who are becoming old are drinking our coffee, taking our vitamins, snuggling into our dressing gowns. What or who is to prevent us from remaining in this instant forever, with the morning papers stretched out before us? What is this relentless power that draws us, minute by minute, into the future, leaving no time for hesitation or doubt? How can we dance to the music that pulls us forward?

"I could leave the world with today in my eyes," Sook tells Buddy in Capote's story, trying to explain how wrong she was about the presence of God in our lives. Sook had always thought she would have to be sick and dying before she saw the Lord. Now she knows better. She once thought that when he came it would be like "looking at a Baptist window: pretty as colored glass with the sun pouring through." Now she guesses that the Lord has already shown himself, breaking through in our everyday lives. She speculates that things as they are, including grass and sky and a dog pawing earth for a bone in the Alabama countryside—just what she has always known was knowing him. It is a message Capote writes down for all of us, a message he remembers all his life.

"Fruitcake weather!" With these words Capote evokes the keen anticipation of Christmas, the turning of the year. Words from Capote's story come back like a refrain, signaling the pull of time. Through the chill days, as our lives turn into winter, we keep moving into the future. It is now that our love of God will be tested. Will we, too, experience the fullness of "today in our eyes"?

SPIRITUAL EXERCISE

Evaluate your spiritual practice as a way of dealing with the later years. Have you flagged in the pursuit of prayer? Are there some practices that appeal to you more now? Or less? Consider what might give you a burst of energy or inspiration. A retreat? Taking up the use of a personal journal? Certain kinds of spiritual reading? Joining a spiritual formation group? Seeking out a spiritual director? Recognize your own obligation with regard to the spiritual life, and consider what changes may be in order.

QUESTIONS FOR REFLECTION

- Have you noticed, as you get older, that spiritual life is different for you? How so?

- What kind of commitment have you made to prayer? What other spiritual disciplines are important to you?

- Do you engage in the prayer of requests, that is, petitionary or intercessory prayer? Have you tried contemplative prayer? What new prayer approaches would you like to try?

- As you get older, what are the nagging issues in your relationship to God?

- How does a prayer group or a Christian friend help and encourage you in prayer life? What about books that may lead you deeper into spiritual formation?

- Reflect on the seven moods of prayer just discussed: beginning, yielding, darkness, transparency, fear of heights, spiritual friendship and clinging. Can you relate to any of these? How?

NIGHT FEARS

Some Things We Are Afraid Of

Everyone is afraid of vulnerability, of falling. Losing one's dignity is only the half of it. No one wants to lose control.

So when I began to take care of my mother in her last days I was shocked when she had a fall. She had fallen at the breakfast table, from her customary chair where she sat every morning to read the paper. In reaching for the second section of the *Times-Picayune*, only a few inches beyond her fingertips, she slipped entirely from the silky upholstered dining room chair. Now she lay flat on the floor, looking upward at the ceiling and laughing. Her cane was stretched out beside her. I was also laughing, but inwardly I was afraid. It took a few moments to get her up, to reestablish her dignity in the spot she generally occupied. From that location she could resume giving orders: "I need the sugar. Please bring me a spoon. I need the ice in this glass to be chipped smaller than this, and please bring me a second glass with just water, very little ice, filled to the top. Also I need my

vitamin." No sound of the word please anywhere. After a short
silence, there came an embarrassed thank you.

Immediately, as if to refute this distress, a second scene
flashed to mind: an image of my mother completely in command. I saw her in a fashionable taupe wool coat, smart gold
earrings, black kid gloves crushed at the wrist, a handsome
dark wool dress, imported calfskin shoes and handbag. She
was, in my imagination, still the ideal CEO, completely in
charge, Helen to many, Mrs. Dietrich to everyone. Even to me
she remained "Mrs. Dietrich" in my imagination. I knew her
as the person who founded companies, launched ventures, develops the potential of employees, hatched creative business
proposals and ideas. Now that she was aging, slipping, she was
still "Mrs. Dietrich" to the bank executives, lawyers and CPAs
with whom I had to deal in her behalf. Never, I thought, could
I fill her shoes. Even on the checkbook she was "Mrs. Helen
Dietrich"; I was simply "Emilie Griffin." No one could dis-
place this towering figure in my imagination. Though she was
merely five feet two, she was larger than life; she reigned.

"I think in your mother's next career she should become
Queen of England," said David Bendix, her former court-
reporting associate, as we sketched out plans for a party in her
honor to be held at the New Orleans Board of Trade. David
was partly spoofing about Helen's membership in a number of
hereditary societies; but mostly he was acknowledging her capacity to wield the scepter, on most occasions, with high humor and a kind of glee. Helen had style. The Dietrich dazzle is
unmistakable, I reflected once again, knowing that for me the
name and the business enterprise she founded in the tourism
field will always be one and the same.

I was the one in denial; Helen was dealing with her old age

better than I; I myself was fighting against not only her old age but my own.

It became clear to me, as perhaps it had not done before, that everything would have to change. My mother's apartment would have to be sold in order to satisfy the mortgage and pay debts. My mother would need to move in with us, but that would require some engineering, possibly some adaptation of our rooms. Would we need a special chair-fitting for the staircase? Was other work needed? My mother would not be restored to independent living again. And my husband and I would not be able to pay the mortgages on her home and our own, while affording help for her at the same time.

STEERING THROUGH TEMPTATION

Less than an hour later, as I rummaged through the library books to be returned, I found this passage in Doris Lessing's novel *The Summer Before the Dark:*

> Kate sat under the tree in such a way that her body was in the shade, and her legs were stretched into the sun as if they were stockingless. She was examining her large square house in its large garden. She did this like someone saying goodbye, but that was only because she and her husband had recently been saying that now the children would soon be altogether grown, it might be time to start thinking of getting themselves something smaller? A flat? They could buy a house in the country and share it with friends—perhaps the Finchleys.
>
> Kate often thought about this, but as of something that was years off.

The passage made me thoughtful about temptation in later life. In Lessing's novel Kate is an older Englishwoman who goes to work as a language interpreter for an organization called Global Food. Her assignment takes her to a conference in Turkey. There she decides to have an affair with a man much younger than herself, and they travel together through Europe. Meantime Kate's husband is on business overseas, as he often is.

How is it that temptations come to us almost in disguise? Some of us are blindsided by the sexual encounter. It seems to be the height of our experience. When youth is gone, we try to recapture it by fantasizing about casual affairs. Like Captain Queeg with his strawberries, we look to repeat some past success, to relive some earlier triumph. Fiction and romance novels reinforce this impulse, give us chances to repeat the daydream. In reading them we relive the sexual encounter with its high drama and sense of wonder. What on earth can compare with the exquisiteness of the chase, seeking and being sought after? Hearing the other person say sweet things provides some slender reassurance of who we are.

But does it? Doesn't the aging woman with the younger male companion know what falsehoods she is clinging to? Can't she guess the things being said about her behind her back? What about that older gent, glimpsed in the elevator the morning after with that female young enough to be his daughter? Does he really believe his security lies in being sexually powerful? Then, what must he think when that security begins to ebb, when he feels he's not the man he was?

It's easy to laugh at the stereotypes, much harder to see the truth in ourselves. A strange twist of vision moves us in the wrong direction, drives us to sin; sin is hurtful self-wrong, something seized as a good which is in fact not a good but an evil. We are like the storks, migrating from the north of Europe into the Sinai desert, whose bodies are too exhausted to make the full journey. Some inner, migratory survival instinct sends us into an unknown that is unhealthy for us, but it is our own good we are seeking.

Maybe not every older person has to navigate such sexual temptations. The larger issue in our temptations seems to be a loss of control. We want to relive and recapture the times when we were at the center of things.

To navigate these temptations, we must learn to recognize them. We need to release control, to share the management of events with those who are younger than ourselves. As we continue to work in our sixties we may have to report to those in their thirties and forties. If we are attentive to clues in these new relationships, we understand that what we have to offer comes through longer years of living, through insight and wisdom of the later years. We still have much to offer even when we are no longer in charge.

NAVIGATING THE LIFE JOURNEY

How are we to stay the course in each stage of the life journey? Only by grace will we come through; otherwise we too will stumble and fall. To be more truthful, we ourselves have already fallen, yet our falls from grace are not always public; we have managed to hide our little escapades, or we have driven our sexuality inward, hiding it underneath fat folds of repression and denial. No one is exempt from the power drive that leads into sin and self-will. Wherever, whoever we are, we may lose our way. Longing for mastery and power, we want to hold back time. When we are young, we rush to sample the full range of human emotions, afraid of missing something, of having our lives pass without meaning, without event. We wonder: *What if we became old and knew we had missed it all?* Yet in the randomness of casual friendships and affairs, in uncommitted relationships, we find no permanence, nothing to hold on to. Commitment is the only way; if we want satisfaction and safety, we can't find it by a scramble over the wall.

Now youth is behind us; we have shouldered the heavy commitments of maturity; we have come through, carried the load—mortgages, loans, entanglements, debt. At last we see in ourselves and others the signs of old age. How are we now to behave? Are we supposed to spend the rest of our lives doing small tasks, falling asleep in front of blinking television screens with newspapers over our faces? What, if anything, lies ahead? Have we missed everything after all?

At midlife we discovered and developed our spiritual lives; possibly we embraced them so fully that this spirituality of ours became a new form of relentless pursuit; far from a letting go or a surrender, the learning of a new vocabulary and a new way of living and believing took center stage; we gave our lives over to a new spiritual enterprise.

Possibly also we refurbished our dreams. Coming through tough times, we have found our deepest springs of creativity; we returned to the fundamentals of our life ambitions; we remembered and tried to affirm again what we once believed in. This brought a freshness, a renewal. We felt young all over again. Falling in love with God was ecstatic, delirious, intoxicating. This new and passionate discovery took years off our lives.

But as with our first fervor, this second or third fervor of midlife begins to ebb; now in fact we are faced with a life passage that can never be confused with youth. This is the hard slog into a future that does not seem unlimited. In front of us there is a wall, and the wall does not seem to be a wall that we can scale.

A new kind of discouragement plagues me with questions. Haven't I lived my life already? Haven't I plunged deeply into experience, amassing achievements, building friendships, reinforcing family ties, doing community service, receiving awards? Does anything remain to be done? Is it time now to retreat from the fray, to stop trying, to go out in the woods somewhere and find a Walden to rest in? Do I understand or embrace the possibility of rest? Do I regard play and leisure as false paths, inauthentic and empty because they serve no one but myself?

When I cared for my mother full-time I felt captured, caught in time. My future, I thought, had caught up with me. My mother required everything of me. She had to be helped from the bedroom to the bath, to the breakfast table and back again to the big chair. Someone must lovingly bring her the newspaper, the television log, the glass of ice chipped just so, the telephone, the mail. The Lord had engaged me in this service. I was called, I was there to serve, I became part of the scheme. But why didn't I feel the grace of it, the consolation?

That was a spiritual challenge, I realized at last. I had to reflect on the meaning of time. I had to understand why I felt so stuck. Why was this pocket of time different from another? Hadn't every phase of my life been "caught in time"?

I remembered in a rush how it once felt to have young children, to be awakened each morning by a squall. I remembered the long hours watching *Sesame Street*, *Mister Rogers*, the *Electric Company*, *Captain Kangaroo*. When was I ever free? Before I had children, I wanted them; I was assailed by fears that they would never come to exist. Before I had a husband, I dreamed of him, of how he would be, of the life we would build together. I chased him in fear that he might not exist! Always I have been in a dance of commitments not yet made but dreamed of, rebelling against alliances and entanglements already made.

Freedom and Delusion

There's a difference, it seems, between the obedient freedom God wants for us and the rebellious freedom we demand for ourselves.

Almost every day we hear of some well-known person who has betrayed his or her marriage by having an affair, or someone who has betrayed a trust through financial transgression. Bribes have been taken. Dollars have been laundered. Lies have been told. All of it was done in the hope of "getting away with it," and sometimes these sins have been hidden for decades.

Transgressions like these are prompted by a certain desire for freedom or mastery. But this kind of freedom is delusionary.

Even so, I have my own yearnings for freedom. I'm sure they are simply human. I want to be footloose. I want to be that cowboy on the plain who has nothing to answer to except the dogies and the overarching sky: don't fence me in! Yet fast and loose is not footloose. In the fast lane there is a kind of anguish far beyond mine; among those who burn the candle at both ends is a fear that will never be set to rest. My fear is as nothing to that fear. Or possibly, all fear is a kind of death.

"If a man keep my saying, he shall never see death" (John 8:51 KJV). We live not only in a physical space but we also swim in inner consciousness. The only possible human freedom lies in a comfort zone within that consciousness. Freedom comes as a realization that we are loved, accepted, in the deepest sense, secure. Men and women in later life who run scared from a lack of acceptance, trying to find relationships that make them comfortable and set them free, fail to recognize that only one fundamental relationship is every fully dependable and secure. "If God be for us, who can be against us?" (Romans 8:31 KJV). The Lord is near to those who call, supportive to those who know his name. Intimate friendship with God sets us free.

Saddled with painful life circumstances, it is easy to blame God for our woes. The answer to this vicious circle of thought? A breakthrough must be made in the spirit. We have to remember and believe that God's wisdom is greater than our own.

Prayer and worship are ways of facing what is real and true. By admitting the boundaries of our existence we feel less confined. By confronting our sulkiness and anger we stifle their inner tyranny. Acceptance, intimacy with God, lets us break through barriers and limits. Is it because we accept our limits or because we move beyond them? I'm not sure. But I am sure that coming to know God is a move for freedom. It is not so much an escape as acceptance, yielding to God's mastery of our lives; we find ourselves set free not by doing but undoing, by relenting and being just who we are and who God means us to be.

FAME: THE LAST INFIRMITY

One of the false paths is fame. We suppose that by building monuments to ourselves we will elude the tock of time. This commonplace way of thinking is entirely delusionary. Empire-building, whether through dynastic families or in office towers, is often the material of tragedy. John Milton called fame "the last infirmity of noble mind." He knew it was a trap, one that was especially dangerous for outstanding people.

Arranged in cartoon patterns on the cover of a Sunday magazine, the faces of Elvis Presley and Richard Nixon re-

mind us of the hollowness of empires. Massive libraries in
California, massive plantations in Tennessee will not confer
the necessary grace of salvation. It is through God alone that
we pass through prison walls and are delivered from the crip-
pling bondage of time.

> Cast me not off in the time of my old age; forsake me not
> when my strength faileth. . . .
>   But I will hope continually, and will yet praise thee
> more and more. (Psalm 71:9, 14 KJV)
>
> Now also when I am old and greyheaded, O God, forsake
> me not. (Psalm 71:18 KJV)

What about immortality? Mostly it is a confusing idea, in
conflict with our experience of time, confounding the imagination. Recently I was asked if I wanted to do a certain project for
the sake of my posterity. All at once I remembered my daughter
Sarah saying, "You think too much, Ma, about your posterity."

Each one of us wants identity. Each one wants to make a
contribution. In Nathaniel Hawthorne's *The House of the Seven
Gables* a woman is told that she will begin to experience truth
now that she has begun to work for something. But to work for
immortality, for a legacy, for the sake of posterity? These are
false paths and fools' errands, indeed.

It is glorious to watch a film performance by one of the great
dance teams: Ginger Rogers and Fred Astaire. But isn't their
performance chilling at the same time? There they twirl on a
Manhattan roof, captured on film like china figures dancing
together on a music box. Caught in their celluloid immortality,
the great movie stars of the past repeat their performances word
for word, flawlessly, gesture by gesture. If we aspire to a kind

of immortality, surely it must be more than this, to repeat a moment of near perfection over and over. Life is a matter of surprises: but the butterfly in lucite is beyond surprise, immobilized, not immortalized.

THOSE IMMORTAL VISIONS

What sort of immortality do we hope for? Perhaps immortality is the wrong word after all, a leftover from Greek and Roman religions that no one has practiced for centuries. The Norse and the Celts have their own immortal visions: the island of the Arthurian legend swims in the sea off the north coast somewhere, a Bali Hai that may call us any night, any day. Each of us is summoned by our own special home, a dream that blooms on the hillside and shines in the stream.

Resurrection as promised to us is inconceivable. What could it possibly be? Then we shall know even as we are known. We can aspire, at least, to a passionate and dynamic kind of knowing, a resurrected knowing, a beatific knowing, completely flooded and drenched by the love of God. This is a moment we can only guess at from moments of transcendence in the here and now, from human love, from reunions of the heart, from moments of insight, from breakthroughs in forgiveness, from embraces and reconciliations, from moments of high ecstasy in prayer.

Our ancestors took the biblical images at face value, supposing they would be given a pair of golden slippers at heaven's door. Our contemporary jokes about St. Peter at the pearly gates reveal how hard it is to believe that God will keep his promise. "There were three men who met St. Peter at the pearly gates, an Irishman, a Vietnamese and a hippie, and St. Peter said . . ."

Yet the yearning for heaven is very deep. This longing for heaven was never so plain as in a book by Geoff Ryman called *Was*. Knowing my interest in the Oz metaphor, my son has given me the book for my fifty-seventh birthday. Only the slightest glance convinces me that it is a lyrical book about memory and pain. To compound the experience, I choose to read it while waiting in a long line on a hot summer's day at the Department of Public Safety and Corrections of the State of Louisiana. I must wait four and a half hours in line before the officer reviews my proof of insurance and charges me a fine.

In this little purgatory I am swept away by Ryman's imaginative interweaving of Los Angeles, California and Kansas, the intersections of the lives of Judy Garland, Frank Baum, the mystical Dorothy Gale, the historical Dorothy Gael and a man named Jonathan who is dying of AIDS. Ryman persuades me again of what I already know: all country is heart country. John Milton's insight is fundamental: "The mind is its own place, and in itself / can make a heaven of hell, a hell of heaven."

What does it signify to live long? Ryman's longsuffering hero, Jonathan, is thirty-eight and knows he will not live to see the year 2000. To me, as a believer, his emptiness (as with many of the book's characters) seems like a failure to know that he is deeply loved by God. This is the hollowness of the book. Its chilling ironies are jokes against God. Aunty Em's religious zeal is a mockery; Uncle Henry's sexual history is heartbreak; across the American landscape there is no sign of Glinda the Good Witch of the North. These are T. S. Eliot's hollow men and women, their heads and bodies are stuffed with straw. The Kansas wind whistles through them.

"Look, look, he's right over there!" I remember how in my

first days of religious conversion I saw God on stage as the silent player in the theater of the absurd. While Lucky and Pozzo and Estragon and Vladimir waited for the Godot who never came, I saw God's presence in and through them, and wanted, like the child at her first theatrical, to shout from the audience, "Look! You're missing the whole thing! He's right over there!"

How is it that we constantly overlook God? Our unwillingness, our obstinacy, our determination to do it all on our own, without help from Anyone, this is the deep source of our anguish, we are Greta Garbos who want to be alone and then complain that no one comes to call. The deep mystery of our God is his willingness to be present to us even when we are absent to him. "Before they call, I will answer; and while they are yet speaking, I will hear" (Isaiah 65:24 KJV).

DEALING WITH OUR FEARS

There are right and wrong ways to deal with our fears as we move into later life. As we pursue the life voyage, we stop keeping a resume; earning a degree seems less important than receiving an accolade; it is time to do less, to accept the thanks being given for what we have already done.

And what if there are no thank yous? If the birthday cards don't seem to come? For years, not realizing it, I looked for my salvation in the mail room. Letters received were my warrant of real life; then I grasped that I was holding on to one more delusionary satisfaction, one more earthly treasure that ought not to be laid up on earth. Where your treasure is, there will your heart be also.

Sometimes our desires for achievement are a way of dealing with fear. Out of the past, the figure of John Milton, writing epics in spite of blindness, dominates my imagination. I think of Beethoven's deafness. I dream of Einstein's life work.

Does ambition have me in its grip? Do I work to serve or am I in pursuit of that seducer known as Fame? Why must I write the great American something? Is this not also a failure to trust in the providence of God? Yes, I have to earn a living. But do I have to earn salvation as well? No, it is mine as a gift.

Fear is the enemy; sometimes the fearful imagination loses control. When my mother's friend Dorothy began losing her sight, I thought: *What if I lose mine also?* When I learn that my beloved professor Mildred Christian is losing her memory, how do I react? Am I grateful for the years when her prodigious memory was poured out for generations of students? Or do I think defensively, *What if it happened to me? How would I manage in such a case?*

Trust is the issue once again. What kind of a God are we dealing with? Yahweh, I know you are near, standing ever at my side. You guard me from the foe and you lead me in ways everlasting.

The Promise of Forever

What we need most is spiritual courage. We need a biblical imagination to see God as he really is, in all his tenderness and power.

Before us there is a whirlwind, and in the midst of the whirlwind is I AM. I AM to whom all the world yearns; I AM, who yearns for his people with a boundless love. I AM is the one who drives all loves, who guides all paths, who walks before us on the yellow brick and every other road. I AM will give us the heart, the mind, the sense of being full, not hollow, who will satisfy all our yearnings and bring us home at last.

His city is more than emeralds, more than sapphire and rubies; all perfection reigns there; in that city the falsehood of our perfectionism is burned away by the fire of God's enduring love. Perhaps it is true that Dorothy Gael is a child deformed by the old child-rearing methods that seek to break her heart and her will. Yet our God is no such heartbreaker. Ours is no hard taskmaster who tries to break the will of the child; instead, he is a tender father who holds his child in a lap of love, waiting, with infinite patience, for the child's free surrender to grace.

Such is the gentle dialogue between the old one and the child; between a Lord who has always lived, has lived and will live forever, and shares his forever with us. We who are made in his image are also incredibly old; if not eternal, we have nevertheless been present in his mind for a very long time, if not surely from the beginning. In any event the Lord has always longed for us; he has lived for us and looked forward eagerly to our response.

So we are someone, after all. We are not orphans, sent on a long journey into Kansas to an Aunty Em who fails to meet the train; we are not the Dorothy whose fairy-tale clothes are snatched from her by abusive adults with bristles of contempt and pain; we are not unwanted children, left on doorsteps. Our God has not abandoned us.

Our Lord is the one who loved Ephraim when he was a child. He leads us, too, with leading strings of love; he pacifies us with the breast of his tenderness; he stoops down to us, dandles us, presses us to his cheek. Even our sexuality and its transgressions he understands and forgives. *Adonai, Adonai . . .* even in the violent and lawless cities your name is praised: there and here and everywhere you are truly God.

Spiritual Exercise

One way to develop spiritual courage is by attending reunions. To attend class reunions is to learn that some of our number have already died, and others may be in danger of dying soon. What is more critical is that some have achieved more than others, some have lost their looks, others their money or prestige. Reunions require of us that we understand how to let go of harsh interpersonal competitiveness, forgive ourselves for what we have not done and stop counting the dimensions of other people's swimming pools. The Ten Commandments are useful: Thou shalt not covet thy neighbor's mergers or acquisitions. Thou shalt overlook thy neighbor's bankruptcies.

Questions for Reflection

- Is there a particular incident—like seeing an older person fall or possibly taking a fall yourself—that has alerted you to your own vulnerability? How have you dealt with a particular form of denial?

- Can you think of a certain temptation you have resisted? Do you think that temptation was related to getting older? Or can you forgive yourself for a temptation you failed to resist?

- Are there times you feel neglected or "washed up"? How can you overcome these feelings?

- Are there ways that you resist the idea of immortality? How do you think the Christian hope of heaven is different from other beliefs in life after death?

- What can you name that you especially like about getting older?

CHURCHYARDS

The Hope of Resurrection

Growing older is having others die around us; they are our friends, part of ourselves. They have gone ahead to a destiny that is also waiting for us. In Louisiana families make visits to churchyards, putting flowers or greenery on the gravestones and celebrating the lives of those who have gone before. And there are many other ways to remember and be in touch with those who have "gone before us." Creating family albums is one. Even better is showing a family album to someone and sharing stories of those who are still vividly present to us in memory. When we look with eyes of faith, it seems these people who have died and gone ahead of us have become more intensely alive, more real. Our lives are bound to theirs with hoops of steel and with mystical cords of flame.

MY FATHER'S PEOPLE

My cousin Celeste has sent me a group of old photographs and souvenirs from the Mischler-Dietrich family. These are my father's people.

I am unprepared for the emotions I feel as the photographs slip out of the package: waves of memory and not a little pain. Here is my grandfather who died in 1963. In the photograph he is beaming. I remember him smiling over the head of foam on a stein of beer at Kolb's German restaurant. I remember him picking up my mother and father in his shiny black Studebaker as he gives them a ride downtown to work. I remember him fishing in his pocket, almost every day, to give me a bright silver dime or even a quarter to put in my piggy bank. Where is he now?

Through the tunnel of memory comes a remembrance of my grandmother Christine, known as Teen or Teenie to the family. She stands at the top of the steps at the house on Dublin Street; the screen door bangs as I go up for my weekly Sunday afternoon visit. "How are you, kid?" she greets me. She is wiping her hands on her apron. We sit on the front porch and try to talk, but there is almost nothing to say. She calls my grandfather from inside the house: he is asthmatic, often using the breathing machine. I am sixteen, seventeen: it is hard for me to grasp what it is to become old.

My uncle Oliver joins us on the porch. His eyes crinkle with delight when he sees me. Oliver is baffling, an enigma: intelligent, educated, speculative, yet as far as I can see he has no work, no calling, can't sustain a career. What is the affliction that has wounded him? There is a rumor that his life was destroyed by an unhappy love affair, that he has had an emotional crackup; it is not fitting for a teenager to know about these things, let alone raise questions. Clearly, however, Oliver is a weight on my grandmother's heart.

To me, Teen seems flinty hard, yet I know she is passionately involved with God. She is intensely Lutheran. My grandfather has left the Roman Catholic Church for her sake, a perilous risk to take in the understanding of those days. He must have loved her dearly to become a lapsed Catholic by taking such a step.

Out of the box of Mischler family photographs come still more treasures: rolled up papers of great value. Teen's high school diploma, her confirmation certificate, in German; their marriage certificate, beautifully adorned with biblical citations. They have died; they have gone to another place; where is it? Will I see them again, ever?

My faith tells me that they stand before God now and their faces are filled with light.

Teen and E. G., Oliver and his wife, Doris, all are buried in one of those old New Orleans cemeteries where the tombs are white and beautiful and above ground. I have a photograph of my father, standing in front of the Mischler tomb, remembering Teen and missing her. No doubt he is also contemplating his own life and death. Everyone has such moments, walking through graveyards, confronting the mystery of existence.

A HINT OF RESURRECTION

It is hard to think of a graveyard as an entranceway to the kingdom; it is hard to think of a grave as the door. Yet from others, people of faith who went before me, I have learned somehow to believe in resurrection. On my mother's side, the family burying ground is at Grace Church in the small, historic Louisiana town of St. Francisville. I experience a hint of resurrection there. And others who know the place tell me the same: for them it is a place of blessing and peace.

In my mind's ear I hear the voice of the clergyman reciting the

Anglican burial service: "In sure and certain hope of the resurrection on the last day, when the final trump shall sound . . ."

I find myself reliving my own history with this church. All
my life, in my visits here, Nui and Eula and my cousins Henry
and Anna Prescott have been preparing me for the end of their
lives, and for the end of my own.

The year is 1982. My son, Henry, is twelve, but not too
young to be one of the pallbearers for Eula's casket. I see how
he has a sense of the occasion; being part of the group with
other men of the family is a rite of passage for him; he has a
sense of ceremony. At her death, Eula is ninety-two. It is a
good, long life, a life to be celebrated. She has told me on many
occasions, "I've had a wonderful life."

Strength of spirit is hard to describe, easy to recognize. It
can be felt, it is something substantial. Eula and Nui had it;
they knew how to share it; I always thought the Bible had
something to do with it. They believed that the Lord was an
ever-present help in trouble. He would deliver them from
the noisome pestilence. They would be strengthened and
rescued by his constant vigilance. They would be raised up
on eagle's wings.

The spring tea at St. Anna's residence for the elderly is held
in 1993 on April 22. On that same day my mother is honored
at the Board of Trade, in a beautiful reception for the people of
the tourism industry. Because she can't attend two events in
one day (her energy is flagging), my mother delegates me to
attend the St. Anna's tea. Lalita will be expecting us.

The day is overscheduled. David Bendix and I are rehearsing
and revising our presentation for Helen's party at the Board of
Trade. We finish our rehearsal and preparations close to 2 p.m.,
the starting time of the St. Anna's tea. By the time I get there

it is past two o'clock, and I look too much like a business executive, too little like a party guest.

When I go in, Lalita is nowhere to be found. They've taken her upstairs already, I learn. When I pursue her, up the back elevator, I see at last what has been causing my mother's sadness for the past several weeks. Lalita, frail and very old as she is, has been hurt. Her face is black and blue. Has she been abused by one of the staff? Or merely taken a fall? Information is sketchy. No one is quite sure. And on this particular day her physical injury is as nothing to the loneliness she feels.

"I had to come upstairs," she says. "It was terrible. There was a tea and nobody came. Winston didn't come. Helen didn't come." Winston was her nephew, on whom she relied. Obviously, she relied on my mother as well.

After a long time I was able to convince her that I had come in Helen's behalf. After a still longer time she realized who I was.

"Emilie! You're Emilie!" Her face was suddenly alight, in spite of the bruises, her beautiful spirit shining through. "How is Helen, how are the children? Tell me about Lucy, Henry, Sarah. Did you get some sandwiches? Go downstairs again, there are lovely refreshments. I'll wait for you."

Weeks later, three days after her ninety-ninth birthday, Lalita dies. "She was ready to go any time," Helen reminds me. But Helen's heart is also breaking that she was not able to go and visit at the last because of her own injuries and infirmity. What sense does it make? What is it all about?

"The coffin will be closed," Petty assures me. Petty is Lalita's niece; she is eighty-five and must move around in a wheelchair. But when I get to the funeral home, the coffin is not closed. The way things are done these days, Lalita seems only to be asleep, looking beautiful, almost smiling. She seems at peace.

But I am filled with sorrow. Not because Lalita has died; it was good for her to die after such times of weakness, impairment and suffering. For more than a decade she has been completely bent over with severe arthritis. It was time.

I am saddened by the separation. Where is she? When will I see her again? Why does my imagination fail to grasp the passage through the pearly gates? St. Peter in his gown, with his feathery wings in a thousand or so *New Yorker* cartoons, has weakened my religious imagination. Michelangelo's ceilings, his putti, will not do it for me.

Are Eula and Nui and Lalita in Grace Churchyard? Where is this place they have gone? I stand, a child before a solemn mystery, a riddle to which there is no answer, the riddle through which, as Emily Dickinson says, "sagacity must go."

For a time when our family lived in New York City in the Borough of Queens, our apartment overlooked Maple Grove Cemetery. "Doesn't that bother you?" people would say. It didn't bother us; Maple Grove is not anonymous, no overcrowded metropolitan burying ground. In Maple Grove I often experienced peace. From our apartment window we saw birds, trees, snowfalls, gravestones. On certain days it was part of our walk to the subway. On this walk I once wrote a poem called "Faith."

It is as though
in the haze over Queens
and the sun blazing through it
I could see the face of God.
As though in the blooms
of rhododendron-bushes
(albeit choked with empty cans)
I could adore Him.

Even the graves
as I pass
shout to me
God is Life,
and there is grace
scattered along my path
as I reach for the subway-token
in my pocket.

IMAGINING THE LIFE TO COME

All efforts to imagine death and the afterlife fail, leaving us feeling foolish and confused. It is simply beyond us; there is, as the Victorian writers used to say, a veil beyond which we cannot see.

I am gripped by a fear, suddenly, that all religious storytelling in the world is delusionary. The moment in the Oz story comes to mind when Dorothy and her friends find the little man behind the curtain, pretending to be a great wizard. Even the words, in all their whimsy and humor, came floating back: "Pay no attention to that man behind the curtain." How, then, am I to be comforted? Consolation is a human invention, meant to lull us past our fears!

Is death an illusion? A passage into a new dimension? Is it possible, as some suppose, that a vast company of the blessed looks back toward us, rooting for us, praying for us, encouraging us in our struggles? In Thornton Wilder's play *Our Town*, those who have already died sit on folding chairs to represent a graveyard. They comment on and understand our struggle, but they are beyond it; they have moved, as it were, to another level of consciousness, where the things we bleed for no longer matter. When Emily, the central figure of the play, dies and joins them,

she is young. She has, perhaps, not let go fully of the attitudes of
her former life; she has not fully embraced the life to come. "You
know as well as I do," Wilder's stage manager explains,

> that the dead don't stay interested in us living people
> for very long. Gradually, gradually . . . they lose hold
> of the earth . . . and the ambitions they had . . . and the
> things they suffered . . . and the people they loved.
> They get weaned away from the earth—that's the way
> I put it—weaned away. And they stay here while the
> earth part of them burns away, burns out; and all that
> time they slowly get indifferent to what's going on in
> Grover's Corners. They're waitin'. They're waitin' for
> something that they feel is comin.' Something impor-
> tant, and great.

Wilder's theology is shaky. He says they are waiting for "the
eternal part in them to start coming out." Where is the blazing
light of God, lighting up every crevice of those who have gone
before us? His insight is animated, perhaps, by belief, but something less than biblical. Emily Dickinson comes closer when
she peeks through sagacity's riddle:

> At last to be identified!
> At last, the lamps upon thy side,
> The rest of life to see!
> Past midnight, past the morning star!
> Past sunrise! Ah! What leagues are there
> Between our feet and day!

THEY HAVE GONE AHEAD OF US

There are days when those who have died and gone before me

seem vividly present, as if they were beside me in the room, like Clarence the angel in a Jimmy Stewart movie, trying to earn his wings. The intimacy of my relationship to my grandmother seems to grow now with each passing year. I think of Eula strongly on certain days, at certain times. Recently I stumbled on a voice recording of Eula and two cousins of mine, Cornelia Cabral and her daughter, Cornelia Quinn, visiting in my mother's living room about family stories and history. To hear their voices, all speaking together, was startling. Two of the four have already died. Yet they were so alive! I thought, now they are even more alive than that. A poem by Henry Vaughan celebrates the friends who have died, who have "gone into the world of light." He misses them and feels he has been left behind by the joyous company of the blessed ones:

> They are all gone into the world of light
> And I alone sit lingering here.
> Their very memory is fair and bright,
> And my sad thoughts doth clear.

Henry Vaughan's poem is on fire with belief in the more intensified life of those who have gone ahead of him:

> I see them walking in an air of glory,
> Whose light doth trample on my days:
> My days, which are at best but dull and hoary,
> Mere glimmering and decays.

Vaughan goes further. He speaks of death as something beautiful.

> Dear, beauteous Death! The jewel of the just,
> Shining nowhere, but in the dark;

What mysteries do lie beyond thy dust,
Could man outlook that mark!

For Vaughan, death is a liberation. Our intense starlike identities are captured now in a prison of sorts, but death will release them.

If a star were confin'd into a tomb,
Her captive flames must needs burn there;
But when the hand that locked her up gives room,
She'll shine through all the sphere.

How different from the pagan notion of eternal life! For the Greeks and Romans the immortality of the soul was something endless, but not always satisfying. The story of Tithonus, who asked the gods for eternal life but failed to ask for eternal youth, is a case in point. With their usual enjoyment of human misery, the gods of Olympus granted his wish without rectifying his oversight. Tithonus grew older and older, his immortality was burdensome. At last, he was so aged that his voice became a squeak. In the end, the gods took pity on him and changed him into a cricket!

By contrast, we believers look forward to transformation, a change that begins here and continues hereafter. The new Jerusalem is one vision of this fulfillment. Since childhood I have loved this imagery in the book of Revelation. Mahalia Jackson makes it vivid when she sings about a vision of the Holy City: "Jerusalem, Jerusalem, lift up your gates and sing!" More naive visions come in the songs of gospel churches and spirituals of times gone by: "Who's that yonder, dressed in red; must be the Israelites that Moses led; who's that yonder, dressed in white? Must be the people of the Israelite."

When I myself wanted to trace a vision of the kingdom, I used the small Louisiana town of St. Francisville as my poetic figure. The vision came to me, as a sudden recognition, through a breakthrough in understanding. Like Sook, who understood that the Lord's presence is already with us in the things we already love, I came to see the presence of God in this small country village so dear to my elders.

St. Francisville was for me a mystical place, revealed to me by the storytelling of the old people I first loved. Through them, I thought I could reenter the past and find a door to heaven along the country path.

"Tell me the story again about twisting the wild horse's tail."

And they would tell me again.

"Tell me the one about Billy and the rattlesnake."

And they would tell me again.

So that when I wanted to spin the vision of a place of perfection, of resolution and completeness, I could hardly find a better place than St. Francisville.

St. Francisville is a historic Louisiana town that enjoys its own history. Each year the town celebrates the past—especially the early 1800s—with an event called the Audubon Pilgrimage, named in honor of John James Audubon, who painted both birds and people during his brief stay there. In my family St. Francisville was linked to a golden era, a time of family solidarity and perfection that had been lost (four generations before) when we pulled up stakes and moved to New Orleans. My grandmother and her sisters often told stories about their childhood in the town and its environs. (But when they spoke of the town, they more often called it "the country.") For me these memories belonged to an idyllic, mythic past. But also, because our family burying ground was at Grace Church in St. Francisville, it was

associated with people—people I had never known but who
were very much alive in the family's memory.

The novelist Walker Percy contributed to the metaphor as well.
One of the subjects we covered, during a long visit I had with him
and his wife, Bunt, was the meaning of St. Francisville, where
both he and I had family ties. "St. Francisville is an enclave, you
know," he said, teasing me about whether I could be buried in the
Episcopal cemetery after deciding to embrace Roman Catholic
faith. Since he himself had made a similar passage, the joke, he
seemed to think, was not only on me but also on him.

People who live in St. Francisville bristle when you tell them
it's an enclave. Maybe it isn't, anymore, but Walker Percy was
not wrong in remembering its exclusiveness, its clannishness,
its small-town just-us-folksness, and a high romanticism about
who our people used to be. All this, I saw, would be part of my
religious vision of the elect. St. Francisville was the perfect
place to symbolize the heavenly kingdom.

After I had my long visit with Walker Percy, my mother
wanted to know if I had reminded him that we were kin to the
Percys. I hadn't even remembered that we were. And if I had
known, I wouldn't have dared to mention it.

After my grandmother's death I wrote two poems. One of
them, "Homecoming," described the arrival of the funeral cor-
tege at the town of St. Francisville.

> When we came to Alexander's Creek
> I thought
> she's home now.
> And when you said, turn there,
> that's the way to Troy,
> I thought of her

running, as a child,
no shoes on,
grass between her toes,
twisting the wild horse's tail.
We were all home, then.
But she most of all
having gone home
a whole day ahead of us
long before we came
to Alexander's Creek.

People who pray a great deal find that the boundary between here and hereafter grows thin, like that kind of theatrical curtain called a scrim. This almost transparent drop sheet reveals a new scene behind the scene which is already illuminated downstage; it creates the effect of an epiphany, a revelation. Now we are like members of the audience who see only what is downstage; later, or when our consciousness is heightened through intimacy with the Lord, we will see beyond the muslin curtain the blessed who have gone before us, and they are about to break into the opening number of the show.

A song from the Broadway musical *Gypsy* tells us we are headed for stardom; we have nothing to hit but the heights. Another moment in the theater that always strikes me as a metaphor of heaven comes in the show *A Chorus Line*. Throughout this musical, characters are seen mostly in rehearsal clothes. As they tell the story of their personal ambitions and struggles, they are speaking also of a dream of perfection that can't be achieved here and now. In the closing number, which is really a curtain call, all cast members return, now in glittering attire; in top hats they execute the most difficult and dazzling numbers. This is a foretaste of bliss. Then we shall know even as now we are known.

OUR NEED FOR METAPHOR

The religious imagination is the way over and through the bafflement that lies ahead. In a time of great sophistication we reject the imagery our ancestors used; it is too naive, too simple-minded, too storybook for us.

Yet metaphors are needed. The Lord speaks to his own in every age and breathes into them the inspiration they need. By intimacy with God we are lighted up; an illumination lets us see the ancient metaphors as speaking to us. Death is a mystery; we can't decipher it; we do not know what we shall be. But we know death as a corollary of time; and we know that even that time we think is given to us is not guaranteed.

Reason enough to live in the present moment, dwelling in the presence of God, treasuring the instant we have against the trials still to come; but faith that moves mountains is greater than this; genuine faith knows that the times to come are all prefigured in the moment that is. Experience scatters like raindrops across the pane; prayer unifies yesterday, tomorrow and today. It is time to yield to the structure of experience, to accept the reality of time. Wanting to be masters of the clock, the calendar, lords of the universe, we resent our situation. Why has no one consulted us about the timetable? Were our proposals and preferences not taken into account? How could the Lord have neglected to ask our opinion about the way he has written the rules?

But we experience an inward change, a kind of melting, a necessary yielding to the pattern, and this is the real pursuit of happiness. Enough of chasing through multiple worlds for power and prestige!

In their simplicity the gracious old challenge us to being rather than doing. They praise God by being who they are, not seeking to justify his affections with a list of accomplishments to date. Part of our own task, as we get older, is to cherish our inheritance of faith from those who have gone before us and who help us to wait patiently upon the Lord.

SPIRITUAL EXERCISE
Organize, if possible, a significant journey.

I was moved by a newspaper account of a woman who took her aging mother on a journey through Europe. She took her mother from a nursing home in the Midwest and took her along on a complex European journey. Though her mother's memory was failing and she could not retain memories of, or even perhaps fully appreciate, places she was passing through, what mattered was the companionship between mother and daughter. It was a holy journey and an opportunity for the daughter's spiritual regeneration. "Then again, her thoughts would drift into places I'd never before heard her mention. For example, she told me how on some summer mornings when she was a child, her father would hitch up the horse and buggy, the kids would pile in, and they'd all drive out to a spot called Mint Springs, at the foot of a hill that mounted steeply all tangled with mint and other greenery. A kind of paradise, she remembered." The mother and daughter were not religious. Still, it seems that they knew about paradise! Especially when her mother says, "I'll bet Mint Springs is standing just as it was somewhere around here."

QUESTIONS FOR REFLECTION
- How is the religious imagination a blessing in dealing with our fears?

- What have you learned from family memories? Including people you loved who have died?

- What specific places help you to sustain the hope of resurrection?

- The Bible is rich with metaphors. Why do we need metaphors?

- Are there elements in literature and art that give you glimpses of the resurrected life? Can you name one of them—a painting, a play, a piece of music—that helps you to sustain your faith?

WEAVING
FAMILY RITUALS

A Word About Letting Go

How do we handle our family lives as we come into the later years? When the heavy obligations of our forties and fifties drop away, can we explore reality in a new way? Can we let go of the anxiety of parenthood? Can this later life passage lead to new creativity?

There seems to be a connection between family storytelling, holidays and the necessity of letting go. Christmas is often the focus of this—possibly Thanksgiving plays a role too. These are the holidays when families gather, even if they are now scattered and live far away.

ANCESTORS

"You're down-nesting," my son Henry explained as my husband and I outlined what we thought we might want to do with the Prytania Street house for the future. He made this remark when we were considering whether my mother would move in with us. We were certainly restaging our lives. But another change was taking place: Henry had moved out, but without letting go of his collecting privileges and without fully vacating his room. We wanted him to stay, but we needed to renegotiate our relationships as adults. His devotion as a son was part of what sustained us and gave us hope; we wanted to see a lot of him for the fun of his presence and his light conversation. How would we decide what films to see if we couldn't consult him? How would we know what novels by younger and established writers are worth reading? Even so, we wanted him to have his own life, separate from ours. This was true with all our grown children.

How were our grown children handling this transition? Lively and imaginative people, they knew how fragile our lives were, that one day we too would be gone. They watched us grow old before their eyes; our limbs were stiffer; we complained of new ailments; we were obsessed with our work, with completing the task. Clearly we were in a time of change. They stood by helplessly, not knowing what to do, laughing with us, encouraging us, pointing out our failings in joking fashion. Birthday cards, gifts, loans, patience, favors of one sort or another, these are the ways they show their love. We knew we were rich in having their affections, seeing their achievements, sharing their hopes, friendships, aspirations, even their sadness, their losses, their confusion.

"What are Helen's ancestors doing in our living room?" With this startling question Henry once revealed to me that he had not yet accepted his Southern past. My mother had given us the family portraits that had always hung in her living room.

These nineteenth-century folks in formal dress took some getting used to once they looked down from our walls instead. The women wore Spanish combs and black bombazine dresses, and had camellias in their laps. The men sported crisp white Wordsworthian collars and their noses were red from a London night out on the town. (And then we had another ancestral challenge: the portrait of Sarah Jennings Churchill, first Duchess of Marlborough, said to be our forebear as well.) Such vestiges of high birth and the heritage of the past bore down on Henry's sensitive conscience as they did on mine.

The questions were unspoken but they were real. How can we come to grips with our history? How can we deal with the sins of those who did not even recognize their sins? Was it good to honor our ancestors? Or did it place an extra burden or obligation on us?

"White? It means nothing to me. When they say 'I'm Italian,' 'I'm Jewish,' whatever, I get upset because I can't really say what I am. I am an African-American, I'm just a black person in America," says twenty-seven-year-old Robert McGriff, a New Orleans teacher and counselor, interviewed in the New Orleans *Times-Picayune*. "I can't even claim the continent of Africa, because I don't know where exactly I came from. I don't know whether I'm Kenyan, or I'm Zulu. I don't know if I'm from Morocco. I don't know."

Through Christian belief I have found an answer that satisfies me. We are all the children of God through baptism into Christ Jesus. "There is neither Jew nor Greek, there is neither bond nor free, there is neither male nor female: for ye are all one in Christ Jesus," says Paul in Galatians 3:28 (KJV). He goes on to explain the adoption as sons and daughters that we have all experienced through Christ Jesus. "And because ye are sons,

God hath sent forth the Spirit of his Son into your hearts, crying, Abba, Father. Wherefore thou art no more a servant, but a son; and if a son, then an heir of God through Christ" (Galatians 4:6-7 KJV).

The genealogy that should most concern us is our spiritual descent from Abraham and our inclusion in the broad and generous covenant between God and humanity. Yet we worry about who we are and where we have come from, tracing our family histories through the baptismal registers and family Bibles and marriage certificates on the civil rolls.

Is there any harm in cherishing our ancestors? Surely there is much to praise in the work of hereditary and patriotic organizations, those who build monuments and lay wreaths to remind us of worthy and sometimes forgotten causes. Drenched in family history on my mother's side, where a sense of lost nobility was always somehow lamented, part of the myth, I had to wrestle with my working-class history on my father's side, where few records were kept and hardly a photograph remains. "High birth," Eula quoted to me once, "was ever in the mind." She attributed the saying to King Alfred. Don't we all, on some level, long to believe that we are meant to rule? Our faith tells us that we will come into that inheritance. Royalty is part of the promise, not a human royalty that is subject to losses, rivalries, conspiracies, political whims, but a royalty of the spirit that can never pass away, a royalty that is possible to anyone who is faithful to the promise he or she receives.

STORYTELLING GIVES US HOPE

Perhaps the best thing about family storytelling is the way that myths are spun, myths that commemorate the betrayals of the past, the chicanery, the double-dealing, and myths that exalt

our forebears for their courage in adversity. In each family
there are patriarchs, who, like Moses and Aaron and Miriam,
lead us out of the land of the Pharaohs and out of the house of
bondage. For my mother, my grandmother, for Eula and the
rest, these patriarchal figures were Papa and Mamma. If they
had human failings, we never heard about them. Instead we
heard how they had lost their land in St. Francisville, but never
looked back. They moved to New Orleans to make a new start,
raising five children and becoming revered figures in the family and in the neighborhood. These were people who won
through in perilous times through strength of character and the
capacity for hope. I tried to capture this thematic storytelling
in three prose poems, titled "Louisiana: Three Recollections."

Plantation child
running with fat legs
along the dust brown path,
patting with pink toes
over the bridge,
the creek,
down by the bayou's edge:
you are eighty now, and more.
You hold the needle out,
peer for the thread,
remembering ghosts:
Mamma and Papa and Uncle Sid
and mules to ride on,
pulling the wagon,
turning the gin,
and I look up, listening,
dreamy heart, dreamy eyes,

trying to think it was I,
blackberry pickin'
with black lisle stockings
stretched over my hands.

■   ■   ■

If I had a coat of arms
I would have wisteria,
rampant.
As I first saw it grow
where Mamma's house was:
just a black chimney now.
The fire took it.
Do you know she had king-snakes in the house
        as pets?
Only country folk could sleep there,
those who loved wild things, unafraid.
When she was old,
Feltus, the man of all work
who lived on the place,
got the old car to sputter,
drove her into town.
She's gone, and so the house is.
But the wisteria throngs and climbs over the
        token-fences.
For what fence could enclose Mamma's wild things?

■   ■   ■

Mamma lived at Troy;
Papa at Forest.
Oh, no, not my Mamma.

My grandmother's Mamma.
Everyone called her that.
I would have, too. But she died.
My grandmother kept her thimble in the sewing-box.
And everyone recalled her.
In the faded albums
She was just an old lady.
Frumpy black dress, stout tummy, practical shoes.
But cameras twist. Photographs betray.
I could trust memories more.
Mamma, who never looked back when the plantation went.
Not for taxes really.
Something worse, cousin selling cousin
down the river.
Into the land of Pharaoh.
Papa was brave, too.
Everyone said it.
Do we have Papas now that everyone believes in?
God, please let me be like Papa and Mamma.
Your humble servants of Troy and Forest.
Just this I ask in Jesus' name.
Amen.

WEAVING FAMILY RITUALS

One of our best strategies at this moment in our lives is the conscious weaving of family rituals. No doubt this is part of the parents' desire to hold on to the younger generation; as such it should be carefully questioned and scrutinized. But on another level our family rituals are part of a desire to pass something on, something precious that exists at the level of memory and story. These are the jewels of our experience that have power to make our children more free.

I remember how I tried to evaluate what was distinctively ours in family life. What would we treasure as the unique voice of our common relationships? How did we celebrate Christmas in a specially Griffin way? I began to treasure, for example, one of Henry Griffin's holiday affectations: that of hiding gifts around the house (perhaps this began in his early childhood with Easter eggs) and then writing humorous clues so that we could find them.

Lucy, I noticed, was especially good at planning and writing cards and notes; funny birthday cards seemed to be her signature. Sarah's contribution to family life seemed to come in terms of order; Sarah from the beginning has brought her gifts of social reform into the family circle. When I was unable to make order in the kitchen because of painful work overloads, Sarah began to create the perfect kitchen, at least in her mind's eye. In her neat handwriting I found lists of needed groceries, of spices on hand. Gradually from these clues I began to spin my own conceptions of what might hold our family together in the scattering of our mature lives.

CHRISTMAS: OUR YEARNING FOR PERFECTION

Christmas leaps out at me from the albums, a metaphor of family closeness and also a reproach. In the staged photographs of my own childhood Christmas, I know and remember a kind of falsehood: my parents were on the verge of a breakup, which the photographs don't show. Our yearning for a Christmas of perfection is a yearning for what is not yet, a something we can dream of but can't fully possess.

The familiar rituals, the lights, decorating, preparation, filled as they are with confrontation and anxiety, are in some ways representative of the feast. Yet we want to live Thanksgiving and Christmas out in a spirit of prayer; the holidays call us to hope that dreams come true.

As I get older, I anticipate Christmas. I seem to be planning, or at least dreaming, months ahead. I have a sharper sense of what the festivities mean. Perhaps it is the loss that I know I am dealing with, the loss of family life as it has been, the casual, unplanned visiting and exchange of conversations, even the buffeting and the arguing have become dear to me.

The reflective spirit turns everything upside down and inside out. Christmas is not a time of lavish bounty but of inner fasting; we are poor and we know it as we wait for the birth of the King. Among the tinsel and the glitter, the catalogs brimming with extravagant options, there is another spirit at work: a spirit of simplicity that wants the power of the manger story to flood our hearts. We want to be open to Christmas that makes sense on a deeper level, in ways we can't explain.

One of the reflective exercises I have pursued and recommended every holiday season is praying Mary's prayer, called the Magnificat, through the four weeks of Advent. This is a historic season of preparation for the birth of the Lord and also for the final coming of Christ. More to the point it asks us to become ready for Christ to enter our hearts. Mary's prayer, prayed throughout the season, helps us to develop mindfulness, a reflective, even a contemplative spirit. It is a prayer said in search of biblical wisdom:

> My soul proclaims the greatness of the Lord,
> and my spirit exults in God my savior. . . .
> For the Almighty has done great things for me.
> Holy is his name. (Luke 1:46-47, 49)

When we become fully mindful, as Mary was, both of the power of God and of our own powerlessness, we approach the holy season of Christmas accordingly. We understand how much there is in the world that we would change if we could, but we are powerless to change. We decide, fully, to surrender to the Lord's working in our lives, and at the same time we learn fully to hope for the coming of the kingdom here and now.

This kind of prayer, tied to a season, which carries us through and into an event—praying through Advent toward Christmas, or through Lent toward Easter and beyond—reminds us of how particular our lives are, how we are creatures of time. By imagination we can become even more connected to reality if we ride with Mary on her journey from Galilee to Bethlehem, waiting to bring the Christ child to birth. When we make such a spiritual journey with vivid imagination, we come across our own impatience. We are faced with a longing to get on with it, to conclude, to arrive somewhere, to know that our time has been well spent, that the time we are spending is not spent in vain.

We want to know what we, who are Mary's people, following in her footsteps, can actually do in our own lives, what we can accomplish against this enormous weight of sadness that we feel. And we want to know how we can adequately bring joy to others, to bring Jesus to birth in our own lives and in the lives of others, in a city and a country torn by violence and exhausted by fear.

What can we do? What can anyone do? We can hope.

Hope is the child that Mary bears. Hope is the child we too can bear, in our thoughts, in our actions, in our lives.

MYRTLE: WHAT SHE MEANT TO OUR FAMILY'S CHRISTMAS

Myrtle wasn't related to us, but she made a difference in how we spent our Christmas and some other holidays too. She would show up at our doorway, sometimes with a borrowed supermarket cart, looking for a little something. And we would always honor that, though sometimes in a pretty modest way. We kept thinking about how Jesus wanted us to give a cup of cold water in his name.

Myrtle was part of our faith life. Because of some of the twists of the social structure in the South, we had to believe that even though Myrtle came to our doorway asking for things, she was not precisely a beggar. Myrtle was a person who believed that the promises made to Israel are true.

Myrtle seemed to expect a kind of justice. She supposed that between the people she knew, and the government of the United States, and charitable places like Kingsley House, and the city of New Orleans, that though she was old and infirm and didn't have all her own teeth, that everything was going to be all right.

Myrtle is the person the Lord has sent to us to be a vivid reminder of God's presence in our midst. She announces in a somewhat irritating way (she rings the doorbell very noisily, and with high expectations) that the poor who trust in the mercy of God and in the kindness of their neighbors are under his protection. They are Christ's poor, they are my poor, and I am responsible for them.

Now there is another voice in me that cries out, "I am powerless." Myrtle better take care of herself, because I have nothing to give her. Myrtle, for me, is that woman bothering the judge in the middle of the night till he got up and gave her justice.

Myrtle is for me, in Hebrew phrase, the *anawim*, the powerless person in the vast, shredding cloth of society, here and everywhere, that reminds me I must care.

John Baillie, in his book *Invitation to Pilgrimage*, has this to say:
"The Bible everywhere encourages us to believe that those who
work for righteousness are allying themselves with his almighty
power and can count on his support, while those who work for
evil are his enemies and have his power against them."

All through the wars of the Old Testament, Israel is not spoken of as winning the battles, but God. "Thus God that day
humbled Jabin the king of Canaan before the Israelites" (Judges
4:23). After the battle was finished, Deborah proclaimed in
song that "the stars in their courses fought against Sisera," who
was Jabin's commander in chief. This is, Baillie insists, the old-
est piece of Hebrew literature extant, the Book of the Wars of
Jehovah.

This theme is pervasive throughout the Old Testament.

Some trust in chariots, and some in horses: but we will remember the name of the LORD our God. (Psalm 20:7 KJV)

Through thee will we push down our enemies: through
thy name will we tread them under that rise up against us.
For I will not trust in my bow, neither shall my sword
save me. (Psalm 44:5-6 KJV)

The Lord of hosts proclaims,
"Israelites and men of Judah are trampled down
         together;
their captors hold them fast, and will not let them go.
But theirs is a strong champion, his name is the Lord of
         hosts;
he will take their part, and daunt the Babylonians, that
         the world may live at peace."
(Jeremiah 50:33-34 Moffat)

Except the LORD keep the city, the watchman waketh but in vain. (Psalm 127:1 KJV)

Baillie asks what right the Israelites had, and what right we have to believe that God is on our side. The answer, he solemnly insists, is that

we can count on having God on our side only so far as we are on his. The question is not whether God is allying himself with us, but whether we are allying ourselves with God. But whenever we do ally ourselves with him, we have the full assurance of his providential help.

This abiding hope in the justice of God is what we express when we pray with the mind of Mary. Mary's simplicity and reflectiveness help us to believe, with a serene and childlike confidence, that roses can bloom in December and snow can fall in July. The faith of the simple heart tells us that even the wasted cities can burst into bloom, at Christmas or any other time, for those who are willing to work for the Lord's kingdom and those who are willing to pray.

Do we have this kind of courage? To believe, as Mary did, that God is working in our lives and that he will overshadow us with his enormous power? Are we willing to make Mary's surrender and believe that good things will also happen today for those who are willing to act for God's kingdom now?

Even when we begin to be wounded by the piercing imagery of salvation, something inside of us holds back, a little voice keeps nagging away. What in the world does this time-honored, sacred tableau have to do with the way we live now?

In answer to this Thomas doubt, words of Scripture come to mind:

Now as he was speaking, a woman in the crowd raised her voice and said, "Happy the womb that bore you and the breasts you sucked!" But he replied, "Still happier those who hear the word of God and keep it." (Luke 11:27-28)

This saying of Jesus reminds us how things really are. What has been nurtured in Mary's womb is our fertility. Mary labors to give birth to the Christ who rules in us.

We are somehow the womb, the creative environment in which Christ's meaning can take hold, be nourished in dark places, grow and swell, breaking open at last in ways that can heal and invigorate our lives.

We ourselves, who are powerless, we who are spiritually and materially needy, we who know the pinch of want, we also know the Lord's generosity to us.

LOSING A FRIEND AT CHRISTMAS

Christmas, falling as it does just a week before the new year, brings a powerful sense of the passing of time.

I shared a "last Christmas" with my childhood friend and classmate Gail Hodges Tranchin, who had been diagnosed with cancer. She was told that she had only a few months, perhaps a year to live. The poignancy of Christmas and its celebrations was heightened for me by knowing it was perhaps Gail's last Christmas. With my usual failure to accept the facts realistically, I sensed her frailty and limitations without fully grasping my own.

Our luncheon circle gathered at a downtown hotel. Across the table, my eyes met Gail's now and then. I had known her since fifth grade. I wanted to say something about what this lifelong friendship had meant to me. But I did not. Instead it seemed better to celebrate being together rather than to speak about the future. I am not sure I ever adequately expressed my affection before her death.

But I saved the place card—a little Christmas tree place card—throughout the long months of the following year. Somehow I was enlivened by her courage, her apparent confidence in the face of death. The small cardboard Christmas tree kept making me think of the holiday brilliance of the Windsor Court Hotel Grill Room, a reminder of the sweetness of friends gathered for the holiday, the circle that will always include Gail.

THE EBB AND FLOW OF TIME

Vita brevis! Life is short, not always sweet. Holidays heighten our sense of the ebb and flow, the boundaries of time. Now our yearning for justice and our sense of being powerless to achieve it is deepened. We must put our trust in Yahweh for all that we aspire to, and be grateful to him for all that we are.

In Mary's prayer, known as "the Magnificat" (Luke 1:46-55), Mary contrasts her humble condition with the greatness of what God has done. Her attention then turns to the extraordinary reversals of divine history, in which God's strength and greatness reduces human pride, might and wealth to no account, exalts those who humbly recognize their position before God and fills the hungry with good things. Mindful of his merciful love, God thus fulfills his promise to Abraham and his posterity forever.

The canticle summarizes the themes of Luke and Acts: concern for the poor and politically weak; for Christian leadership which must not assume the ways of human power; for the quality of Christian nourishment (at the Lord's table); and for the fulfillment of God's promise of blessing to Abraham and his true posterity.

When we pray with the mind of Mary, we will understand ourselves as the true posterity of Abraham. In all the books I write, I have a simple motive: to celebrate surrender and to announce that biblical things do happen. To vouch for my own experience that God is still attentive, even in the twenty-first century, to those of us who pray. I want to use my creative skill to interweave contemporary experience with scriptural understanding, to proclaim with the mind of Mary that the fairy tale of our experience with God is true.

Gail is dead now. She has gone to that other place. I must believe by faith in the ending of the fairy tale, that a magnificent glory is in store for her, that she is entering in to her royal inheritance.

"What shall I give him, poor that I am?" Christina Rossetti asks in her nativity poem. Holidays bring home to us how poor we are, how little we have to show for our efforts. As we grow older we come to the manger empty-handed and our eyes are wet.

In the cradle scene I identify less with the wise men than with the shepherds, perhaps most of all with the friendly beasts who have only their own warmth and affection to give. There is nothing of the world's abundance that can enrich this Child we wait for; he comes to give us the treasure of poverty, of spiritual childhood. That's the reversal of values we most need to learn.

We come naked into the world, but it takes time to understand what we really lack. Christmas after Christmas we grasp our own poverty and see in the beggars and the homeless a reminder of how powerless we are. The kingdoms of the world will not satisfy us; this earth as we know it is passing away; and the new Christendom coming to birth has nothing of empire about it. One must be a child to enter in.

We have heard the carols so often that we don't listen to the words. Yet a deep wisdom is hidden in them. The myth-makers embroider the poverty of the king. "No crib for his bed." "No room for him at the inn." "Once in royal David's city." The rightful king who has come is made homeless by a world that can't assess his wealth. Can we do any better? Can we become rich by his counsels of inner poverty? Only if we are children enough to hear the story freshly, as though for the first time.

All the more reason for praying, even in a time so rushed and hectic that prayer seems impractical, easy to postpone. But it seems there is an unusual depth of memory in holidays. In our holiday reflections we meet, as Scrooge did, the ghosts of Christmas past, present and to come. We have to deal with old memories, childhood recollections of what Christmas used to be. The selves we have outgrown and left behind. That ghost reminds us, too, how much we must hand Christmas on to those who are very young. For their not-always-comprehending sakes we must keep the full meaning of Christmas, even the hard parts. Not just tinsel and glitter, but compassion: forgotten relatives, elderly cousins, needy and forsaken persons too near to be glamorous. And the ghost of Christmas present? That's the one that haunts me with my own fakery, my sudden sense of how little real good I have done. What hearts have I mended? What wounds did I bind up? What quarrels have I soothed? How much have I really loved? And then, forgiving— have I really tried? There are nettles of unforgiveness, clogging my path.

Just in time, on cue, comes the third ghost, Christmas yet to

come. This ghost will stop at nothing to wound my heart! Like
Scrooge, it seems, I have to be converted, just when I thought
I had done all the turning I could do. Am I flexible enough for
this? And will I have enough reprieve to mend my ways, to
send a goose to Bob Cratchit after all? It seems the Lord is using my Christmas meditation as a way of calling me again to a
deeper conversion of heart. It appears he wants me to become
a child again. But how can I become a child when I am old?
And what shall I give him, poor that I am?

Holidays have an ache, a yearning. We are at Bethlehem; we
would be at Jerusalem.

> I know all about you: how you are neither cold nor hot.
> I wish you were one or the other, but since you are nei-
> ther, but only lukewarm, I will spit you out of my mouth.
> You say to yourself, "I am rich, I have made a fortune,
> and have everything I want, never realizing that you are
> wretchedly and pitiably poor, and blind and naked too."
> (Revelation 3:15-17)

We are called again to walk the hard path, to keep Christmas on a level deeper than the storybooks. Time is the bell-
ringer. The Lord himself is the path we walk on, the peace we
are hoping for. Where and what is home for us who have no
place to lay our heads? Holidays remind us that we have no
home, no resting place except in God.

"What child is this who laid to rest on Mary's lap is sleep-
ing?" Before the manger, among the friendly beasts, with our
own children or without them, we know the Child is for us. "I
warn you, buy from me the gold that has been tested in the fire
to make you really rich, and white robes to clothe you and
cover your shameful nakedness. . . . I am the one who reproves

and disciplines all those he loves: so repent in real earnest" (Revelation 3:18-19).

So, Christmas is not only a celebration, but also a time for repentance. We see that we are the needy children starving for grace. "Look, I am standing at the door, knocking. If one of you hears me calling and opens the door, I will come in to share his meal, side by side with him. . . . If anyone has ears to hear, let him listen" (Revelation 3:20, 22).

One way I experience Christmas spiritually is through the prayer of that most enthusiastic convert, Ebenezer Scrooge: "Assure me that I yet may change these shadows you have shown me, by an altered life. . . . I will honor Christmas in my heart, and try to keep it all the year. I will live in the past, the present, and the future. The Spirits of all Three shall strive within me. I will not shut out the lessons that they teach." God bless us, every one.

Letting go is a good way to celebrate Christmas, and essential for the later years. "Generative care," according to the psychologists Evelyn Whitehead and James Whitehead,

> is able to let go, to release without bitterness, that which has been generated. But this mature letting go applies not only to the works of our hands but to our very sense of self generated over the previous decades. Persons are more than what they do, more than the sum of what they have become.

The Whiteheads say that for many adults this is a fleeting insight. It is more than that to me.

We are more than our accomplishments! We are more than our achievements. God does not love us because of what we have done but because of who we are. Our transformation, our growth in grace, comes from yielding, from acceptance. The lilies of the field do not toil and do not spin.

ANOTHER KIND OF HOLIDAY

One thing has been crucial for me: letting go control over holidays. Christmas deepens for me as I get older, but I am less in charge of celebrating the holiday. Along with my grown children and grandchildren, my husband and I conspire in the celebration. We contribute, but we do not oversee.

It is the same sort of change I noticed in my mother during her later years: becoming more flexible, even childlike. In our later years we are more willing to be children. We learn to relax into a somewhat improvised schedule, to welcome change and surprise, to "go with the flow." It is a brief, stressful and sometimes prayerful time of year. Best of all is the joy of being together. And then of course, there is Jesus: the reason for it all

SPIRITUAL EXERCISE

Reevaluate, renovate and restage holidays. Holidays are, in my view, the most perilous days in family life. These are the times when parents most long to possess their children, stuffing them back into the teddy-bear costumes they once wore. A spiritual exercise may consist in asking the children to plan Thanksgiving or Christmas and accepting their suggestions with enthusiasm and creativity. Assess your own weaknesses and strengths in the new relationships by the simplicity and understatement you bring to the new situation of having grown children (whether or not they live away from home).

There's a corollary to this exercise. Make deliberate efforts to let your children go.

Choosing new ways to visit with them as peers, over the

lunch table, at the coffeehouse and the like emphasizes the new framework of the relationship. This is not the same as "down-nesting," encouraging your children to move out. The delicate, difficult and most desirable goal is a renegotiated relationship with children as adults. Recognize how much you have done that they must forgive you for. Forget it, forgive it, move on.

QUESTIONS FOR REFLECTION

- Have you considered ways to renegotiate relationships with the younger generation in your life?

- How do holidays offer a chance to renew and restage relationships? Should all generations play a part in weaving family rituals?

- What about family storytelling? Is this a good or a bad thing in your family? Do some members of the younger generation love to hear the old stories, while others resent it?

- How do you experience Christmas as a window into past and future?

- Does the Jesus story sometimes get sidelined at Christmas? What can you do about this?

A DIFFERENT WISDOM

Living the Cross

One of the best and hardest things about spiritual life is the way it opens me up to the cross. It isn't so much that I choose the cross. Instead, the cross chooses me. The edge of reality pushes in and I know how powerless I am. I am vulnerable. There are things to face that I want to run away from. Something is asked of me that is more than I can handle, it demands more strength than I have.

The cross is the beginning of a different wisdom: seeing the world from Jesus' point of view. And that can happen most any time if we are open to it. Sometimes though, a spiritual exercise, a walking on purpose with the Lord helps me to share the cross in ways I don't anticipate or plan.

C. S. Lewis puts it well: "The Cross comes before the crown, and tomorrow is a Monday morning." Sometimes it is in the sheer Mondayness of things that I experience the cross. Often in our everyday lives we feel impoverished, pinned down. Even if I have goods and resources, I feel that I'm not really free. Something is binding me, there's an anxiety that cuts straight through everything, reminding me that things are out of whack. It's partly my own weakness, but it's everyone else's too. There's the weariness of putting one foot in front of the other, not to mention some other "slings and arrows of outrageous fortune." Someone I know is dying of AIDS. Still another friend who dies "wills me" his loneliness. I realize he died almost friendless and alone. All around me are signs of limitation: boundaries I didn't wish for and can't change. There is no way out but straight ahead. Liberation sounds like an empty word unless Christ is the way.

Oddly, it is freeing to enter into the story. With Christ, in Christ, I can pass into a deeper reality, but only when I am willing to make the walk to Calvary myself. I like that passage in Isaiah that says the suffering servant wasn't good looking. "The crowds were appalled on seeing him—so disfigured did he look that he seemed no longer human" (Isaiah 52:13). It's hard to recognize a Savior when he's powerless, worse off than we are. This is the part of reality I don't want to admit to myself, that suffering is the way in. "Without beauty, without majesty we saw him, no looks to attract our eyes; a thing despised and rejected of men, a man of sorrows and familiar with suffering, a man to make people screen their faces." I have to admit I'm inclined to forget who Jesus is and how to let his sacrifice cut into my life. "He was despised and we took no account of him" (Isaiah 53:3).

Yet, if I live the story out fully, I also have to be among the soldiers who divided his garments; I have to include the part where I give him vinegar and ask if he is really the King after all. If I'm honest, I have to be all the actors in the drama, play-

ing every role to the hilt. I have to demand that Barabbas be
set free instead.

At least this honesty is cleansing; the denial, the whipping,
the scourging, the mocking, all are part of my divided self that
loves the Lord and denies him, turns around and looks the
other way. I have to be both Judas and Peter. When I'm living
the story I'm also feeling the rejection Jesus felt. "By force and
by law he was taken; would anyone plead his cause?" (Isaiah
53:8). And yet we also read just before this: "Harshly dealt
with, he bore it humbly, he never opened his mouth, like a
lamb that is led to the slaughter-house, like a sheep that is
dumb before its shearers" (Isaiah 53:7).

In my own life, it is sometimes clear that the more Christ is
with me, the less I am a comfortable person to know. My simple
choice to belong to Christ may bind me to some people, but it
separates me from others. That is part of what hurts about the
Christian life, we don't ever fully "fit in." When I am in the
marketplace I can't escape noticing this difference. Really living
as a Christian, I don't always feel better but worse, because the
prevailing culture exerts such a pull. Even when others don't
understand me, I have to love them anyhow, doing my part to
help them feel at ease with me! If I live my life unself-consciously
I might be doing some good. I can even forget about it. Then
some chance remark reminds me I'm walking by a different
path, making commitments that others find hard to handle. One
interesting twist to this experience is those unbelieving friends
of mine who love me even when they don't grasp my commitment to faith. This is a kind of trust for them as well.

Yet the surprise of this trip to Calvary is that there's something at the end of the road besides death and suffering. I can't
seem to get there by applying a theory of the cross. "By his

stripes we are healed" has a practical meaning. But I have to follow, one step at a time, to sense that there is something else in store. Just when I think the glory of the resurrection is very unlikely, I find myself standing in the garden with Mary Magdalene after all. Suddenly, where I least expect it, he is alive and calling me by name.

> Jesus said, "Mary!" She knew him then and said to him in Hebrew, "Rabbuni!"—which means Master. Jesus said to her, "Do not cling to me, because I have not yet ascended to the Father. But go and find the brothers, and tell them." (John 20:16-17)

As unlikely as it seems, we do find him in the moment, as Mary did, or the disciples on the Emmaus Road. We see him in the stranger at the table, in the chance meeting, in the love that floods our hearts, yet causes pain. The Lord seems closer when we stop pretending to be powerful and admit how wounded we are. Then he seems to come to us, crucified and risen. When we are honest in prayer, the Lord can catch and embrace us, he can hold us tight. We touch him. We grasp him. To this real Master we cling, this vulnerable Lord with the wounds still open in his hands and side.

A HARSHER TRUTH

It used to be commonplace to talk about our "crosses," the trials and burdens of everyday living we couldn't walk away from or forget. The phrase was, "We all have little crosses to bear." But becoming open to the cross is somewhat different from that. This is the tension that seems to split existence in two. At moments we sense it. We recognize the harsher truth that underlies everything. It is an invitation, yet one we're not so eager to accept.

When we surrender, we too are marked with the painful tension that scars all reality. The world is maimed, distorted, out of whack. The time, as Hamlet says, is out of joint, not just for one generation but all generations. But Hamlet misses the mark when he supposes he was born to put it right. There is only one who can put it right and he has already done so, bearing the tension, the division of existence in his body, so to speak. Not just at Easter, but always, the mystery is played out in history as one, once-for-all event: the Son pouring out his blood for the Father and for us, sending the Spirit to bind and heal us once and for all.

I think we grasp this reconciliation for ourselves only when we are willing to undergo the cross, not just romantically but practically in the way we live. Are we shouting too much? Drinking too much? Giving way to the peer demands and pressures around us? Just ahead is the path we should be walking, the footprints painfully clear. Are we walking with him, yielding to what he asks? Or are we forgetting, denying, not living for him but living for number one?

Some days in the Christian calendar are chances for a change of direction. They prompt us to a specific glimpse of Jesus Christ.

> Across the littered streets
> falls the long shadow of the Cross;
> And over the Manhattan sky
> I see his face
> Thrown back in suffering.

My own poem, written several Good Fridays ago, reminds me of how I can touch the Lord in the pain and poverty of city places.

Just beyond me
A small procession
Moves through Jerusalem streets.
I too am on my way to Calvary.

How am I living the cross? If I can't feel the edge of it in my consciousness, then the fullness of reality is lacking. I need to lean into Christ's presence, accept to the storm he stirs up in me. I have to relent and die with him to be sure of knowing how to be alive. I have to open my heart, my consciousness, to see him, crucified, changing the meaning, transforming the event. There, just beyond the cross, in the sky getting darker hour by hour, I can see the outline of the universe, God designing everything, and us, for himself, to be swept up into his flaming heart.

Is the way narrow? How are we supposed to enter in? We do it by consenting, leaning into the particular, feeling the nails in our hands.

"Do not weep for me, daughters of Jerusalem."

He knows the outcome.

Master, how can I thank you for this gift? This depth of vision that lets me live your story, knowing it as my own? Do I value enough the pearl of your existence? Of knowing how to walk to Calvary with you?

How can I deal with the mystery that is Easter, the death that calls us to live? In the surrender of one man the broken pieces of existence are made whole again.

GIFTS FROM THE SEA

I write this from mid-ocean, not knowing my way. My directions are unclear. My supplies are running short. Darkness is darkness. I know what it means to be at sea.

I can't help thinking that an experience of darkness can never be fully staged. We can't really orchestrate an experience of emptiness; it's not a matter of chosen hardships or fasting. Wilderness is always impromptu, a gift that comes out of nowhere, without rehearsal or warning. When a real desert experience sets in, there's no time to prepare. We're up against it. Trapped in a place without comfort, without support.

Things that fed us before don't seem to nourish us now. We have had to let go of certain dreams for our careers, our attitudes toward fame and achievement, our sense of importance and being in charge. Now we ask, "Who am I? Where am I going? Why don't the plans and dreams I had yesterday add up? Isn't there a structure, a design I can cling to?" The map doesn't match the circumstances. We're going in circles, exhausted, lost. Now's the time to grumble, to tell Moses and Aaron they've betrayed us. This experience isn't playacting. The lines we memorized don't work for these situations. "Why did we not die at Yahweh's hand in the land of Egypt? . . . As it is, you have brought us to this wilderness to starve this whole company to death!" (Exodus 16:3). As so often, when dealing with God, he seems to have changed the rules. We're inclined to tell him he's not playing fair. "Why did you bring us out of Egypt? . . . Was it so that I should die of thirst, my children too, and my cattle?" (Exodus 17:3-4).

Wisdom Comes When We Look Back

How do we handle a desolate experience? A desolate experience—an experience of alienation or darkness—can be seen as a gift. But that is something we realize only after the fact. When we're in the middle of things, our vision is dim. We can't see where we are. This alienation isn't a spiritual exercise that can be scheduled when it's convenient. It rarely seems to coincide with our plans. Accepting the downs of our existence is rarely easy. Instead, we think, *How can I get out of this? How can I move forward in the spiritual life, even though I'm stuck and have no sense of what is going on?*

Maybe the Israelites' story has its own answer coded in. The manna that was sent was barely enough for each day's need, no grace left over for the day to come. (He did send an extra supply to tide them over the sabbath.)

Each day's anxiety has to be lived in trust. That's theory, not practice. Are the shortages meant for my growth? I can't see it. (My gravest temptation is to stage manage everything, write the script and demand that God play his assigned role.) Instead, I need to hold on minute by minute. The more we hold on, give in, the more the actual moment hollows us out. By a gift of imagination, we endure, we grope, we tough it through. "We do not know where you are going, Lord. So how shall we know the way?"

In the blush of my first enthusiasm for the spiritual life I once wanted to take on penances and deliberately chosen fasts. Then my spiritual director counseled me wisely: "Better the penance that you don't choose." Now that I have come into such a place, a place not of my own choosing, it is painful even to remember the false heroics of my earlier plan.

In the past I volunteered to help those who had to stay put. As a lay minister in my New York congregation I became a regular Sunday visitor to nursing homes. In a sense, I think I was trying to compensate for the ways I couldn't be attentive to my own family, living far away. Whatever my intention, I saw a lot of anguish, people trapped in loneliness with less-than-adequate care.

Yes, it was a generous act; yes, it was worth doing. But some of that overenthusiastic ministry seems to me now less than holy, an effort to take center stage in a publicly Christian way.

How much better to stay put and stand toe-to-toe with my own challenges. Now I am fenced in as they were; now it's not so easy to voice my Christian enthusiasm. Now I can't romanticize the experience of tending the sick. Now I see that I am not "caring for the elderly" but becoming one of the elderly for whom others must care. My impulse is to make a break for freedom, for irresponsibility, to cut loose from being the good, obedient child.

Living the cross is giving ourselves when we have nothing to give: breaking, for a moment, the whine of the TV, the drone of conversation behind the hospital curtain. This is an unidentified location somewhere between Horeb and Sinai. We live in hope that tomorrow's manna will fall, as promised.

I know it is time to drop all my disguises, the ways I hide from God. "Down in the dust I lie prostrate: revive me as your word has guaranteed. . . . I have chosen the way of fidelity, I have set my heart on your rulings. I cling to your decrees" (Psalm 119:25, 30-31). A new role has been assigned to me, one that gives me a chance to be vulnerable and open, hour by hour, day by day. Whatever time of year it comes, this is my Lent, an undressing, a stripping off of assumed and false identities. In another sense it is also its own drama or play: our acting out of Jesus' ordeal in the wilderness. Putting on Christ, as Paul says, is dressing up to be like our Lord.

I am called to walk through times of confusion and doubt, keeping my eyes fixed on the Jesus who walks just ahead. Time to ask again, Who is this man? What is he calling me to? And why do we care about him so?

> You did not see him, yet you love him; and still without
> seeing him, you are already filled with a joy so glorious it
> cannot be described, because you believe; and you are
> sure of the end to which your faith looks forward. . . . It
> was this salvation that the prophets were looking and
> searching so hard for; their prophecies were about the
> grace which was to come to you. (1 Peter 1:8-10)

How can we grow beyond our fears in the aging process?
Only perhaps by yielding to that experience and keeping a
sharp eye for God's guiding presence. Angelic sentinels and
guardians can protect us from ourselves, our own deepest fears
and anxieties, our nagging fear of change.

THE PULL OF THE FUTURE

We can almost feel the passage of time; the future pulls us
mightily on. Because we have lived longer, we hope that things
are changing for the better, but we doubt it. We pray for a
political and spiritual awareness that can befriend us in uncertain times with ways to interpret present, past and future. We
hope for perspectives to help us look a hundred years in both
directions: where we have come from, where we are going
after a lifetime of accelerating change in knowledge and
thought. We want to connect with the past and future in a
continuum of belief. We want to be like Einstein's "observer"
and his time traveler who by moving at the speed of light remains young.

What political changes we have seen! Our lifetimes have
spanned the Cold War. We have lived through religious re-
alignments and watched Eastern and Western coalitions re-
emerge. Sometimes it makes us rather weary. We wonder

whether political and social change is merely cyclic, fearing that when things change, they only stay the same. Though we are getting older, we want to plunge into new quandaries. The emergence of spirit in many zones, the stacking of conscious-ness upon consciousness, worldwide planetary anxieties that well may unify the human race—all these things have brought to the forefront religious concerns that at mid-century were often dismissed as beside the point. Once again, it is the best of times and the worst of times, the age of incredulity and the age of belief. Clinging to the Word and the work will hold us steady through sea changes that lie ahead, long after the print-ing press is a memory and our whole history has been con-verted to a computer chip.

"Growing older is a phenomenon which is a common de-nominator for all of us," writes Sister Marie Lenihan, who has devoted many years of her life to work with older persons. "As one enters the latter years of life, activity becomes less possible and the scope of our lives more limited. We come face to face with the reality of our own dying process."

And living process!

"Those of us who have the tremendous privilege," she con-tinues,

of continued contact with people who are now in the frail stages of life, can see their virtues. We see their centered-ness in God, their resourcefulness of facing life's difficul-ties, their emotional maturity and ability to view situa-tions with a positive outlook. Each person develops these characteristics to a greater or lesser degree because of his or her life experiences, choices made and personality makeup. Many persons at this stage in life have wisdom that only life experience can bring, and a faith that can strengthen and support those around them.

These qualities sustain the people as they grow older.

Consider a poet who in old age became still more visionary: Alfred, Lord Tennyson. In his mind's eye the future held great wonders as well as great uncertainties. Tennyson, in his eighty-first year, not long before his death, wrote about the last passage in high nautical style.

Sunset, and evening star
And one clear call for me
And may there be no moaning of the bar
When I put out to sea.
But such a tide as moving seems asleep,
Too full for sound and foam,
When that which drew from out the boundless deep
Turns again home.
Twilight and evening bell
And after that the dark!
And may there be no sadness of farewell,
When I embark;
For though from out our bourne of Time and Place
The flood may bear me far,
I hope to see my Pilot face to face
When I have crossed the bar.

Tennyson's phrase "no moaning of the bar" is based on an old superstition. The outgoing tide sometimes moans as it rolls over an intervening sandbar. This was once believed to mean that a death had occurred.

In a memoir Tennyson explained who the Pilot was: "that

Divine and Unseen Who is always guiding us." A few days before his death, Tennyson asked that this poem be printed at the end of all editions of his poems. For me it has in it the sound of the evening bell, telling the time at sea, insistently, as the vessel moves into the dark.

SPIRITUAL EXERCISE

Tell stories and hand on traditions. Be sure that in the development of family rituals, you include the creativity of the youngest members, and allow for activities that will amuse them. Consider what will entertain and attract them about your past and their past. Especially try to make connections with distant relatives. Become a letter writer if you can. Include, in your writing, to the extent that it is natural and appropriate, your faith in God. Your letters will become a spiritual journey for yourself and a spiritual gift to others

QUESTIONS FOR REFLECTION

• How do you experience living the cross?

• Can you identify with "the Mondayness of things"? If so, how?

• Have you experienced darkness and doubt in the middle of the life journey? Do you think of this as an experience of the cross?

• What is your internal response when you read of the poet Tennyson's desire to meet his Pilot face to face?

EASTERING

Transformation in Christ

I learned the word *eastering* from Gerard Manley Hopkins. In his long poem "The Wreck of the Deutschland," he uses it to speak of Jesus Christ:

> Let him easter in us
> Be a dayspring to the dimness in us
> Be a crimson cresseted east.

It was the first time I had ever seen the word *Easter* used as a verb. Of course, I knew it was a word of Anglo-Saxon derivation, because the word for Easter in Romance languages is different. In Latin the word for Easter is *Pascha*, in Spanish it is *Pascua* and the word comes into English when we speak of the "paschal mystery." I assumed that Hopkins had taken hold of the word *Easter*, a Christian holiday focused on resurrection, and invented a new way of speaking about how Jesus Christ enters into us and transforms us.

All of that was true. But later I learned that Hopkins did not invent the word. It was a nautical word in common use to mean "steering one's craft to the east." By "eastering" Hopkins meant to convey steering toward or turning toward the light of the resurrection. Of course, all the Easter imagery is about darkness and light. In the Easter vigil service, just as it becomes dark outside, the Easter fire is lighted and the flames whip high in the spring winds. Then the procession comes into the darkened church and proceeds down the nave holding the Easter candle and singing "Christ Our Light." As they move down the center aisle, those in the pews light their small candles too, until the darkness of the church is illuminated by pinpoints of small lights. All this is to remind us of the light of Christ.

When I enter into the depth of the words *Easter* and *eastering*, the beauty of the resurrection breaks over me again. Christ is our light against the darkness of death. As the light rises in the crimson-cresseted east, we celebrate his rising once again.

All this in a single word! Not only that, it makes perfect sense. For Hopkins's amazing poem "The Wreck of the Deutschland" is about faith transcending death. His long poem is a cry out of the darkness, an effort to understand and accept the mystery of death. The poet's anguish is prompted by the death of five Franciscan nuns who died when the Deutschland went down off the Welsh coast, who died with the name of Christ on their lips. In this poem as in many others, Hopkins wrestles with the mystery of suffering, with the seeming injustice of death. But finally he accepts what he cannot understand. As the long poem rises to its final crescendo, Hopkins speaks to God:

> I admire thee, master of the tides,
> Of the Yore-flood, of the year's fall,
> the recurb and the recovery of the gulf's sides,

Eastering

the girth of it and the wharf of it and the wall;
Stanching, quenching ocean of a motionable mind;
Ground of being, and granite of it: past all
Grasp God, throned behind
Death with a sovereignty that heeds but hides, bodes
        but abides.

"Past all grasp God." In my own effort to accept the mystery
of death, these words have become a prayer for me. And when
I used this poem as part of a retreat for Gulf Coast survivors of
Hurricane Katrina, I saw tears beginning to flow, especially as
the word *gulf* brought home to them that the Deutschland disaster and their disaster were somehow linked.

LEARNING TO SEE AGAIN

In a chapter called "The Birth of Vision," in his book *The Management of Time*, James T. McKay expands our understanding of
what it is to see. First he mentions the situation of an eighteen-
year-old man in the Mayo Clinic who has just undergone an
operation to restore his sight. He asks us, and others, to imagine what the young man will see when the bandages are re-
moved for the first time.

To give us insight into the experience, McKay quotes J. Z.
Young, an authority on brain function:

> The patient on opening his eyes gets little or no enjoy-
> ment; indeed, he finds the experience painful. He reports
> only a spinning mass of lights and colors. He proves to be
> quite unable to pick out objects by sight, to recognize
> what they are, or to name them. He has no conception of
> space with objects in it, although he knows all about ob-
> jects and their names by touch. "Of course," you will say,

"he must take a little time to learn to recognize them by sight." Not a little time, but a very long time, in fact, years. His brain has not been trained in the rules of seeing. We are not conscious that there are any such rules; we think we see, as we say, naturally. But we have in fact learned a whole set of rules during childhood.

It seems that the very obvious spiritual changes of the life voyage are our preparation to see something beyond our immediate sphere, something that we can only guess at and which will only later be revealed. It is not only wishful thinking that makes us say our lives are going somewhere. Even without the eyes of faith we sense a progression, a movement toward something. With the faith dimension it becomes almost a certainty.

I say almost a certainty because my own faith is in a God who will always leave something to our imagination, a sea that must be crossed by faith. Then we shall know as we can't presently know. The fullness of knowing can be sensed, can be dreamed of, can be anticipated, can be known by trust. But there is no way to get ahead of the story.

These are the principles of creative seeing that McCay outlines: (1) You are the creator of your own unique elements of experience, therefore you can change them at will. (2) You select and arrange the parts of your sensory impressions on the basis of your past experience. (3) As your experience in any area grows, you can see more in that area (make clearer, bigger and more accurate mental pictures of what's going on). (4) Since your experience is never complete, you can never perceive all of what's going on; you always leave out a good deal in your observations.

The sea changes of later life may open up a fuller, deeper way of seeing. We must relent, release, surrender in anticipation of another kind of knowing, something like the breakthrough of first learning to read, but far more exquisite. Always, our sense of ultimacy shapes what we feel, what we imagine, what we see. We are eastering, turning toward the light.

Another way of eastering is to confront Jesus Christ in sudden and surprising ways. This often happens when we pray, in ways we can't anticipate. I tried to capture something like this in a poem of mine, "In the Garden," written when I was just past forty. The poem compares our prayer to childhood play. It also proposes that Jesus Christ will actually meet us in our prayer.

> Do you remember
> when you were five,
> that moment,
> just before dark,
> when the fireflies winked
> and a beautiful peace
> stole swiftly on,
> and you thought,
> let them not call me in just yet,
> please,
> it is so lovely here, just now.
> And you thought,
> I shall never have
> this unbearable sweetness,
> this joy,
> ever again.
> Do you remember?

Now that I am eight times five
my prayer is like that.
The Lord takes me
into a garden
just at twilight.
His presence is unbearably sweet.
And I pray,
please Lord,
let me stay,
just another moment, here.

And then, he answers me.
Mind you, I don't know quite how.
This, he says, is only a taste
of what will be,
later,
when you come to me
forever and ever.

It takes some faith
to believe in things like that
until they happen to you.
Then, you want to run out into the garden
again and again.

If we are willing to use the religious imagination, we can
enter into a more childlike and refreshing relationship with
God. If we suppress that imagination, we are killing part of
ourselves, part of our human giftedness. If we give way to it,
we are enriching our capacity to experience the heights and
depths of spiritual life. At last we can take the wings of morning and easter in the farthest reaches of the sea.

SURPRISING PRAYER

When we open up to prayer, we are often confronted with surprises. Sometimes I have a sudden and very concrete sense that God is present to me, something almost like childhood experiences of play. Someone's hands are over my eyes. I can't see him, but he's saying, "Here I am." I almost hate to mention it because I know it's completely out of left field. There's nothing I can plan for or anticipate. Even to name it might make it seem available, when in fact it's always entirely possible and at the same time completely out of reach.

A concrete example in my own life: me, on a Saturday afternoon, suddenly bolting from the house with my Bible in hand, fleeing from the ganged-up responsibilities of living. (I don't mean anything too unusual, really, just the layer upon layer of commonplace obligations and anxieties: no personal space, no time for God or for myself.) So then, I light in a place of repose: the front steps of the neighborhood library. Around me, there's a vast lawn with brownish green grass, everything still a bit mucky from the last hard rain, not much comfort in the landscape, but then, as I open my Bible, a sound comes out of nowhere. A piper! The notes are so unearthly, so unreal, I try at first to ignore them.

The intrusion is completely out of whack, not related to my prayer agenda, even remotely. What does this piper have to do with me?

I open my Bible to Hosea 11. "When Israel was a child I loved him, and I called my son out of Egypt. But the more I called to them, the further they went from me; they have offered sacrifice to the Baals and set their offerings smoking before the idols" (vv. 1-2). Somehow the piper steals into my prayer, a haunting sound that's hard to ignore. Does the piper stand for something with

special meaning for me? "I myself taught Ephraim to walk, I
took them in my arms" (v. 3), the Scripture continues. I know
it's a childhood metaphor, but what is the Lord trying to say? I
feel the music bearing down on me, the sound and Scripture
converge in my thoughts. Now I make a new association: the
Pied Piper, leading the children (I'm one of them) out of Hamlin
town. What a radical figure he cuts, there in his ragged garment
with the odd assortment of colors. How much he reminds me
that the gospel power is something the people of the status quo
fail to recognize. The Lord is speaking in riddles that make perfect sense to children, but which adults fail to understand. He's
spellbinding to those with open hearts.

"I led them with reins of kindness, with leading-strings of
love. I was like someone who lifts an infant close against his
cheek; stooping down to him I gave him his food" (v. 4). And
is this same piper, here now in my prayer, speaking to me?
"They will have to go back to Egypt . . . because they have
refused to return to me. The sword will rage through their
towns, wiping out their children, glutting itself inside their
fortresses" (vv. 5-6).

In the Scripture, as in the folktale, the stakes are very high.
The piper is playing for keeps. He expects nothing less than a
full commitment, an honorable bargain, followed through to
the last. And am I willing to walk with him? Into the moun-
tainside? Taking the chance that the great side of the mountain
will close up, and the children will never return?

The most important part of this surprising kind of prayer is
catching the thread and following it, even if the way lies into
rough places and through the wilderness. The prayer of surprises is what happens when we are open, not only to the
metaphors we decide on but the ones that are flung in our

path, impossible to avoid, challenging us, turning us in new directions. "Ephraim, how could I part with you? Israel, how could I give you up? How could I treat you like Admah, or deal with you like Zeboiim?" (Hosea 11:8). It is hard to trust this Lord who is so demanding. Yet if we trust Scripture, we have to take him at his word: "My whole being trembles at the thought. I will not give rein to my fierce anger, I will not destroy Ephraim again, for I am God, not man: I am the Holy One in your midst and have no wish to destroy" (vv. 8-9).

Finally, I turn and steal a look at my real piper on the steps of the library. Sure enough, there is a person in worn jeans and jacket, a cap pulled down over his ears, piping a tune (it's actually "Oh the Days of the Kerry Dancers," but I'm definitely not in Ireland), and he looks more like a street person than a leprechaun. At least I know the piper is not entirely my own invention. The surprise, though, is finding him there, just at that time of special openness for me. I'm tempted to laugh out loud, it's so improbable. At the same time the guessing game is utterly serious. I feel the Lord wants to shake me out of my complacency. I sense the moment as a challenge, almost a reproach: "What description, then, can I find for the men of this generation? What are they like? They are like children shouting to one another while they sit in the market place: 'We played the pipes for you, and you wouldn't dance; we sang dirges, and you wouldn't cry" (Luke 7:31-32).

The light is falling, but the piper continues to play, and the Lord's voice is strong for me in his music. "The mysteries of the kingdom of God are revealed to you; for the rest there are only parables, so that they may see but not perceive, listen but not understand" (Luke 8:10). There are safer prayers, I suppose. There are formulas, things to recite, prayers to go to sleep by.

But instead, because the world is in flames and people of high courage are really needed, I can choose the prayer that opens me up to God's demands. "And some seed fell into rich soil and grew and produced its crop a hundredfold. Saying this he cried, 'Listen, anyone who has ears to hear!'" (Luke 8:8).

In the prayer of surprises I am a child, setting out with a high heart, to find a kingdom of peace and justice: where they will do no war anymore.

LIVING AT PINPOINTS

One advantage of living to be eighty-eight, according to Armand Hammer, is that, when you keep your wits about you, "the focus of your interests becomes pinpoint-precise." Hammer, in his autobiography, *Hammer*, recounts among other adventures his efforts toward world peace and a cure for cancer during the year from November 1984 to December 1985. Something about the grand scope of his ambitions (how many of us would dare hope to put a personal stamp on such solutions?) is almost funny. Nevertheless his sincerity is unquestionable, even if one hopes that Hammer is not just a Peter Sellers Pink Panther character whose amateur efforts could make world diplomacy and scientific exploration worse.

"It is possible to see with absolute clarity what matters and what is unimportant," Hammer confides. "I know what I want to achieve in the time remaining to me, and if my ambitions are larger than many people's, that just means I have to try harder. I can't think of anything better to do with a life than to wear it out in efforts to be useful to the world."

Hammer's dream and his energy are admirable. Surely, if persons at his level of power and prestige were consistently willing to put their efforts into such global aspirations, something good would be the result. The danger, of course, in such high aspirations, is to be tempted to earn salvation, when salvation is ours already as a gift. Works of service, however grand, are merely our ways of saying thanks.

I like what Janice Brewi has to say about wisdom rooted in religious experience in the book she coauthored with Anne Brennan, *Celebrate Mid-Life*. She says that one's life work can become a religious experience, when our whole being is involved in and dedicated to what we want to achieve. She sees work as archetypal. And she quotes Teilhard de Chardin, that astounding contemporary mystic, to support her claim:

"God awaits us," Teilhard says, "every instant in our action, in the work of the moment. There is a sense in which he is at the tip of my pen, my spade, my brush, my needle—of my heart and of my thought." How can we speak of our work as part of growing older when the real task that seems to lie in front of us is letting go of work, letting go of our longing to supervise, to direct and control?

Some of us may pursue leisure. But some of us continue to work, actively, into our seventies and eighties. George Bernard Shaw began his playwriting career in his fifties and concluded it in his nineties. J. C. Penney wrote spiritual memoirs based on his business experience well into his eighties. Maybe it's a matter of physical strength. Possibly it is about intellectual vigor. Anyhow, we want to keep going as our strength allows. We want to contribute. We want to be of value.

It is good to remember that the work of reflection is also valuable work. Eula, my dear Eula, hit a serious health snag when she was in her late seventies, one that required her to leave the home she loved and take up residence in a nursing home. Cheerfully, she occupied half a room, condensing the belongings of a lifetime into relatively few, though the books and papers did seem to overflow.

At our suggestion—my mother's and mine—she bravely, and with enormous powers of recollection, began to write her memoirs! Abundantly, the loose-leaf pages came by mail, written in her large, clear, unmistakable hand, detailing events long past, country childhood memories, memories of young people's gatherings in New Orleans, marriage, family anecdotes, even an account of the Era Club of the 1920s in which she and others had been active for women's suffrage.

God was at the heart of her letting go. That simple fidelity to him, that childlike trust she had known from the beginning became more so in her last years, focused, as Hammer says, to pinpoints. She knew what mattered most.

Eula's pinpoints were intense moments of family feeling. God and family were ultimately the ones for whom she lived, and passionately. As she came closer to ninety she was more and more grateful for the beauty of her life and told me often what a wonderful life she had had.

"To sum up," says the wise spiritual counselor Jean Pierre de Caussade, in his book *Abandonment to Divine Providence*, "we must be active in all that the present moment demands of us, but in everything else remain passive and abandoned and do nothing but peacefully await the promptings of God."

THE CHRIST STORY BLOOMS AGAIN

"Every day will be an Easter," says one of the hymns I learned in childhood. Is every day a Christmas too? From my postcard box I retrieve one that I discovered in the Atlanta airport with a photograph of dark red dogwood blooms. It tells me "the Legend of the Dogwood." It seems that the dogwood, being a firm, strong tree the size of the oak, was chosen for the purpose of the crucifixion. Jesus, nailed upon the cross, sensed the tree's distress and said to it, "Because of your pity for my suffering, henceforth the Dogwood tree shall be slender, its blossoms in the form of a Cross, two long and two short petals. The center of the outer edge of each petal will have rusted, blood stained nail prints. The center of the flower will be a crown of thorns and all who see it will remember." The legend reminds me of the ways we storytellers can experience both crucifixion and resurrection again, and see them flower in our lives. Even when (especially when) historical facts are scanty, devotion thrives on legends and makes the Christ story present to us where we are: in airports as well as on country lanes where dogwood bursts into bloom. The postcard—and the dogwood itself, when I am lucky enough to be present in earth places where it flowers—are reminders to me that we are Easter people. When Gerard Manley Hopkins says we can let Christ "easter in us," he adds something important. This eastering can occur in the darkness of our lives. Christ can be a "dayspring to the dimness in us." Easter is the dawning of a transformed consciousness, a new way of seeing. When we ourselves live the story, new legends burst into bloom.

A year or two ago a woman I scarcely knew asked me to be part of her Maundy Thursdaying. At her invitation I took part in a washing of the feet with others in her circle, a liturgy designed to express their sense of the Easter message. When I took my shoe off and dipped my foot into the basin, I understood the grace of this moment for me—something this younger woman could not have anticipated. How could she have known (having me on a pedestal as she did) that I was so in need of healing? Could she have guessed that I was the one whose gimpy foot had been brutalized by the overcommitment of my life? Her gesture healed me, if not of my limp, then at least of some of my unwillingness to be attentive to my own needs. A small example? Yes. But larger healings and breakthroughs come about through the same loving openness to grace, the same kind of attentiveness to the Lord's presence in our lives. Another friend, a man, is mugged at gunpoint and lives to tell about it. He understands that his death blow is a life blow, an opportunity to live, even a reprieve, a chance to live differently, from now on. What is even more Jesus-like is his willingness to forgive the oppressors; to work for better living conditions for those who go out of their way to kill him.

Suffering as Transformation

As I get older, I speculate about healing on a larger scale. If individuals can be healed through their conscious contact with God, is the same breakthrough possible in communities, peoples and nations? For a long time it has been possible for us in the West to look down from a pinnacle of affluence or comfort at "the poorer nations," to feel compassionate toward the poor and marginalized simply because they were overseas. Now the crumbling infrastructure is upon us, and we are conscious that the whole system which we depend on is at risk. Problematic events converge—poor law enforcement, the drug crisis, racketeering, drug dealing, violence in the streets—to help us understand our peril. We who are already weak and frail must learn sacrifice for the sake of those even more helpless than ourselves. This is our cross, and in this suffering we will be transformed.

By his stripes we are healed. In such a large-scale task, the stripes of the Suffering Servant of Isaiah will become ours. The flogging, the humiliation of our society's predicament, these times of suffering will no doubt be the making of us. But we need a kind of poetic vision, one that comes in the midst of darkness, to see the presence of God among us, leading us along the holy path. We need sprigs of dogwood—in airports, on country lanes—to know that God is eastering in us and that our sufferings are part of our transformation.

I like the way that Paul, writing to the Corinthians, finds metaphors in ordinary experience that disclose worlds of meaning. A little leaven leavens the whole lump. We who are believers have to become the new bread. Our paschal lamb has been sacrificed. We have to celebrate the festival, not with the old leaven of evil, but with the new, unleavened bread of sincerity and truth. Living in the presence of God makes it possible for us to see new metaphors in our experience, metaphors that will change us if we are willing to live them. Dying you destroyed our death; rising you restored our life. Lord Jesus, come in glory.

SIGNS OF RESURRECTION

Emily Dickinson lives close to death. She speaks of it as a neighbor, part of her everyday experience.

> Because I could not stop for death
> He kindly stopped for me;
> The carriage held none but ourselves
> And immortality.

In Dickinson's day death was commonplace, something that happened in the parlor or in the dining room. So too with Charlotte, Emily and Anne Brontë. In the Brontë parsonage at Haworth, one can be told in which precise parts of the room each member of the Brontë family died. Oddly, this nearness to death produced in these believers not despair but a clearer consciousness of the life to come.

But in my own life things are somewhat different. Now and then I find surprises that strike me as hints of the resurrected life. One consoling surprise is that my son Henry so sharply resembles my father, whom he hardly knew. When Henry was two-and-a-half, my father dubbed him "El Rojo" because of his masses of red curls. A month later my father died. There was, over the ensuing twenty years, very little storytelling about him, nothing to make Norman Dietrich as alive to Henry as he inevitably was to me. In his teens, Henry met my uncle Warren, my father's youngest brother, and grasped a bit of what it was to be a Dietrich. Yet, there is no way that Henry could have taken on the nature of his Dietrich grandfather by imitation or a sense of the tradition. Instead, Henry's Dietrich streak came as a revelation to everyone, including himself. We were unprepared for the Norman-ness of the young man coming of age. All at once, it seemed, Henry matured: as raconteur, performer, film enthusiast, comic, debater par excellence, cultural observer and clown.

At first the secret could hardly be spoken. My mother noticed it but wondered if she was the only one who had. Gradually I mustered up courage to mention it. "Do you see it too?" "Absolutely!" What made it so curious was that Henry's coloring—fair white skin and brilliant red hair, worn, often, at shoulder length during the time I speak of—was at odds with the Norman Dietrich of my memory, a man of suits, ties and Humphrey Bogart snap-brim fedoras, preoccupied with cars, tires, carburetors, gasoline stations. When I call up a mind picture of my father, I see him, circa 1940, standing with one foot up on the running board of an old Chevy, his white shirt open slightly at the collar, tie tugged loose, a seersucker jacket flung over his shoulder, his arm moving up to wipe his face perspiring from the Louisiana heat.

Unmistakably, Norman Dietrich was present again in my son: in the opinions, the contentiousness, the love of picking a quarrel, the radical left-wing politics; alive too in the love of dancing, of night life, of New Orleans music; in joining a carnival marching group (racially mixed, mind you!) that calls itself the Furious Five; in strutting, tossing the red hair, laughing, grinning, clowning, hogging the dance floor at Cafe Brazil in the Faubourg Marigny while his friends the Klezmer All-Stars perform; making a living in video stores and pizza joints and coffeehouses while he struggles to become a screenwriter, novelist, film critic, movie director—all of these! Almost at once, everyone saw it: "He's so much like Norman Dietrich!"

Yes, this is Norman Dietrich's grandson! In Henry's voice, his movements, the jut of his jaw, the flash of his eyes, the suddenness of his laughter, the crazy, entertaining skew of his ideas, his love of speculation, his ability to reflect: all these are my father; are they also myself? All along I had been seeing him, as everyone else had, as Bill Griffin's son and almost double. Everyone has seen that from the beginning: the joking, the love of books and reading, the storytelling, the dramatic imagination, the high romantic streak. Now that the cards are dealt out for another generation I see in Henry that the man I married, his father, is my father, too, in some unaccountable way I never saw before.

Where does yesterday leave off and tomorrow begin? In our children we are confronted time and again with mystery. How could this amazing thing happen, that people who are not our-

selves are in some astounding way definitely us? Probably one of
the best things about my father was that he was fun-loving. I
vividly remember him seizing an umbrella to reenact the drama
of my mother's Uncle Sid and his way of walking down a street.
In the same way my father loved to imitate the marching antics
of the Jefferson City Buzzards, a Mardi Gras marching society.
Now Henry lives the dream again, in ways my father's generation could never have imagined. And my father was pro-civil
rights, so much so that he had the house in an uproar constantly
with his "Yankee ideas." Is political liberalism transmitted in the
genes? I would surely have blamed it on nurture, not nature!

Getting older is not only surrendering the past but giving way
to the future. As if in a series of strobe pictures I see Henry at
fourteen, sixteen, eighteen, walking into manhood and the new
maturity that sits comfortably in my mother's parlor, wolfing
down chicken chow mein, conversing with a very new vocabulary ("What's been going on?") riffling through the *New York
Times Book Review*, working up the last-minute cash to pay his
rent, lingering pleasantly, then hurrying away. "He's so handsome!" my mother said after he had gone. The ache in my heart
deepens, as I feel the weight of my dreams for him, my hopes for
his happiness, my gratitude for his love and friendship.

All my children are my friends! *Friends* is a pale word for the
affection I feel, the loyalty they give me, the steadfastness. I am
praying for the strength to loose them, leave them free, drifting
on water like Oscar's camellias, fresh, fragile, very beautiful.
To see my children grow up is to be awestruck. In them I con-
template wonders I could not have invented or created: the
uniqueness of people deeply like me, yet wonderfully themselves, held together by laughter, driven from within by the
power of a mysterious, mostly unspoken love.

ALTERNATING MOODS: CONTEMPLATION AND REFLECTION

In the garden of the Women's Faculty Club on the Berkeley campus, University of California, I find myself surrounded by roses. They are taller than I am. I have to stand on tiptoe to look at them. Big, tall on their stalks, secured by high sticks, their wide velvet petals curl exquisitely. I am sure God must have thought of them: not only the roses but each detail of their conduct, their seductiveness, their queenliness, their desire to compete, brilliant reds rivaling bright yellows, deep pinks with petals that diminish to pale edges; all three varieties standing high and reaching up for sun.

They are outrageous. But over the way from them is an equal outrage: one oversized white hydrangea bloom, ample, balanced to perfection, dozens of small, hesitant, round petals trembling on silly stems, arranged in formal harmony.

I am reminded of Avery Dulles's moment of conversion at the budding young tree on the Charles River. Then a Harvard undergraduate, Dulles came out of Widener Library where he had been reading St. Augustine and wrestling with the question of God. On the riverbank, in what he took to be the tree's obedience, Dulles, in one burst of insight, saw God. The insight was so persuasive that it brought him, that same evening, to pray. What does my own moment of insight require of me? Is my dialogue with the flowers already a kind of prayer?

Not to mention the ferns. They are robust and fresh. A slate path leads down into shade, going where? From my top-story window I have seen a tall man, handsomely suited in blue, descend and disappear, his white hair so coifed that his hairdo proclaims him the servant of fashion, not indifferent to sex, even possibly vain? (What is this place of such affluence that even the scholars are stylish?) I, Sherlock Holmes, say by means of detection that this fellow on the garden path is Narcissus grown old. He likes his reflection in the mirror and though he is old a certain self-conscious desire to please can be seen as he walks. I say this without hesitation even though my eyes from the upper window catch just a snapshot of him. I am old, and still dancing; he is old, and still mincing. What shall I make of this sound of fiddles tuning up that constantly says to my heart that something is not ending but starting? Young or not, love is the energy that drives the universe. Always, even though it be not sex but spirit, the dance is about to begin.

Behind the house a garden, pleasingly round and green, invites the studious heart. Here harmony is, and wholeness, detachment and freedom. In the past I have come to scholarly meetings completely enslaved by my passions, to win, to control, to dominate. Who was I, in that other time? Why should I feel so different now, yet wary that these passions may assault me again. With detachment I can live within the dimension of roses, inhabit the hydrangea's circumference. I can blow and tremble with the blue flowers that bloom along the college roads. With the pyracantha and the ivy I will proclaim the beauty of God. I have grown wise like the palms of Berkeley and Ein Gedi.

Two kinds of experience dominate me now: contemplation and reflection. Breakfasting after my Berkeley conference, I have talked with a clump of scholars about the transformation of society; one of them, a professor of philosophy at Boston College, has given me a clue in my research. From his kindness and the high compliment he pays me in the dialogue, my spirit soars. I am a writer! I am a scholar! My old age will be the crown of life! In our witty badinage I have reminded him that Cato learned Greek at eighty. He has responded, "Touché." I thank God for his reminder of the things I love in scholarship and intellectual life. Cicero's essay "On Old Age" is one of them! The climb I have made up the wearisome steps of my existence, to this point where the years ahead must be the last, this is not sad but serious; filled with meaning, not the hot promise and potential of youth, not the crunch and clatter of middle life, but something more contemplative, more reflective: at the top of the staircase, a small door leads into the upper reaches of Wisdom. In that tower Rapunzel will at last let down her hair.

SPIRITUAL EXERCISE

Write memoirs. And encourage others to do so.

It is an act of faith to write memoirs. As anyone knows who has been interviewed by a younger person about some historical experience from the past, to write one's memoirs is to admit one's own frailty and the time limits of one's life. This requires courage as well as creativity. To do it joyfully is to live one's faith and to set a good example of how to face old age and death.

Besides writing down your own memories, you might also encourage others, including older members of your family, to do so.

If there is someone whose memories you cherish, who can't organize the project, help him or her to do it. Make tape recordings. Plan interview guides. Think up topics to prompt memories. Experience the flow of memory and time as a spiritual gift to you, and to others, through you.

QUESTIONS FOR REFLECTION

- This chapter explores "eastering" as the way Christ works in our hearts. What are some ways that Christ is "eastering" in you?

- Have you had experienced "living at pinpoints"—intense moments of feeling that give you spiritual insight? Can you recall or describe such an experience?

- How do you feel about interweaving Christian experience with fairy tales?

- Do you find it consoling to pray in certain places, in gardens or where flowers are in bloom?

10

HOMEWARD

Celebrating the Present Moment

One way to celebrate the present moment is by making a beautiful space in the week for friends, and visiting. Such a moment comes for Bill and me when we invite our friends Colette and Jim Stelly and Pouff and Richard Jaubert to have brunch with us.

Have we taken leave of our senses? We have decided to serve soufflé! Why such audacity? What would move us to risk serving such a menu to seasoned travelers who go to France often and are of French background themselves?

Perhaps the fact that I am a native of New Orleans gives me courage. I have grown up with good food, and loving to cook seems second nature. Today, the restaurant fare of New Orleans is even more diverse and pleasing than in my childhood. We have created our own cosmopolitan cuisine. Cooking at home gives me a chance to celebrate this culture, to share the riches of my own heritage. Also, when money is tight, as it is for two writers who are stretching to cover life commitments, having friends in makes it possible to have the elegance of a great restaurant in one's own dining room.

So we have invited good friends (neighbors!) to Sunday brunch. Colette is actually a professor of French. Her doctorate, earned late, is in the teaching of languages. She goes to France often, sometimes taking Pouff along with her; they know both French and Louisiana cuisine well. And their husbands are equally critical! Richard, Pouff and Jim are genuine Creoles. Richard and Pouff are New Orleans natives (her real name is Marie-Elise, but everyone calls her Pouff) who have traveled in Europe often. Jim, a native of Opelousas, comes from a French family that has been in Louisiana at least two centuries. He has lived in New Orleans most of his life and works as a travel agent, with many opportunities to see the best of English and European life.

I, on the other hand, am an American of English and German descent, whose only pretense to French cooking is a lifetime of reading *The Joy of Cooking* and various books by Julia Child.

My motive is clear: something in my character loves to live on the edge. Making soufflé is a kind of pirouette in the hot glare of center stage, a risk-taking bid for deafening applause. Looked at another way, it is my quest for perfection, a high celebration of the beauty of created things. Soufflé is a theological statement, a religious affirmation. God is good! Le bon Dieu has given us the imagination to create soufflé.

Perhaps, also, the house we live in demands soufflé, as it demands flowers and civility in profusion. Ours is an old house, a raised Creole cottage that has weathered many hurricanes. The ceilings are sixteen feet high. In the front of the house is a long, beautiful room, previously a double parlor, no doubt, with high windows overlooking the street and side garden. In this room are two fireplaces. The walls are deep red and the draperies a sort of bone. On the walls are oil portraits of my Louisiana ancestors, Nathaniel Evans, Lucy Adelaide Foley and her daughter Lucy Adelaide Evans; Nathaniel Evans is alone in his portrait, wearing a high formal collar of the early 1800s; family tradition has it that his picture was made in London, after he made money as a Louisiana cotton planter and returned to his native country.

WHERE THE HEART IS

What is the occasion? We are in search of Sunday. All through the winter and spring we have been forced, by the economics of our lives, to work all seven days of the week, believing all the while in the importance of Sunday as the Lord's day. Yet we are working to keep this beautiful house and our lives in it from being swept away. What could be more important, then, than Sunday at home, Sunday with dear friends around us, Sunday with a menu that honors their friendship in some celebratory way.

My husband is the one who loves to set the table and to see the house appointed with flowers; the books that generally overflow in every corner of library and living room must be gathered into some sort of pattern, not too accidental, not too planned. We decide to use our wedding china and silver, our crystal glasses. Bill has chosen a good Chardonnay and has chilled several bottles of Perrier as well. He plans the music also, choosing from our somewhat antiquated library of long-playing records a few that seem just right.

I have the presence of mind to put all the ingredients out, bringing my eggs, milk and cheese to room temperature. The guests are invited for noon. At eleven o'clock I begin to be afraid of running short of cookies to serve with the fruit that Colette is bringing, of time to prepare everything well. I try to send Bill to the store for the cookies I have in mind. He refuses to go. "What if they don't have what you're looking for? You should be the one who goes," he insists. I see it his way and hurry to the store, where I pluck the extra head of lettuce, the croutons, the shortbread to accompany the fruit compote Colette will bring. Bill was right. In fact, the store no longer has the brand of cookies I wanted, and I spend precious minutes looking for others (not too expensive) that will measure up to the meal.

Returning to the house, breathless, I become a quick-change artist, slipping into a dress proper for both cooking and visiting. I discover that the apron is as much a part of my costume as the dress. Part of my joy on this beautiful day is the preparing. Anticipation is as precious as fulfillment.

Separating eggs takes skill; it delights me to discover that even when time is short, I do this well. Gradually, the whites collect in one deep bowl, while the yolks build up in another. I congratulate myself for being beyond the newlywed's hesitancy. I know how to cook!

Over the flame the heat of the double boiler is measured, dependable. With a wooden spoon I stir the butter and flour together, gradually adding the cheese and milk, and feel the exquisite drag on the spoon that means it is just right. In go the seasonings, dashes of salt and cayenne. Now the yolks create a golden texture.

Quick, beat the whites till they rise, fluffy and firm. I find myself remembering a former colleague, a master of the soufflé, who believed the whites should always be whipped by hand. I don't have the elbow strength, don't have it now, didn't have it then! But a terrible thought strikes after I have put my beater into the whites. What if I failed to wash the beater after beating the yolks? What if the whites don't rise?

From the front hallway, I hear the guests arriving. Bill knows that if I don't come out, it means I'm still coping with the kitchen. By now, it's a balancing act. Salad greens being washed, shaken dry, drained, broken into appetizing bite-sized pieces; juicy red Creole tomatoes, the best of the season, quartered; green onions cut; croutons added. In a large glass salad bowl, every color in the salad glows with life and appetite. I pour three different kinds of dressings into my favorite serving pieces: one is the mayonnaise dish we got as a wedding gift almost thirty years before.

But the egg whites! This is my crucible for today. If the egg whites don't rise, there will be no soufflé. The beater whirs and whirs but I see no hope. The sticky mixture lies in the bowl, mocking my aspirations. I add cream of tartar, hoping for the ideal chemistry. Still, no apparent progress. Finally, as the beater keeps purring, it occurs to me to pray.

"Oh, I'm sure Emilie will come out and say hello in a few minutes." I hear Bill making small talk in the front rooms. I'm so glad my husband is a first-class wit. I am sure he will keep everyone thoroughly amused while I continue struggling with the egg whites. Bill is not so much a raconteur as a wicked man with a punch line. His humor, both in his writing and conversation, is known far and wide. Lucky for me in my struggle with the egg whites.

At last, they do rise, doubling and tripling under my astonished gaze. I begin thanking God, as I pour the yolk mixture in, then fill the soufflé dishes and slide them into the oven. Again,

I have forgotten to preheat the oven soon enough. I'll have to trust God to compensate for the oven temperature as well.

As I walk from the kitchen to the front of the house, the joyful sound of small talk falls on my ears. Pouff and Colette are telling their husbands that Bill and Emilie were brilliant in their recent talk. We bask in the approval they give us. Bill serves me a chilled Perrier. I am starting to relax and appreciate camaraderie. On a chair near me, beside the fireplace, Colette's deep pink straw hat, brimming with outrageous flowers, symbolizes all the joy and civility I aspire to. Pouff and Bill are engaged in one of their high tweaking sessions. I know that when Bill is teasing her about the antiquarian charm of the ladies' club she belongs to; he is secretly planning to use the club in some short story or novel he will write! From the kitchen, I hear a reassuring sound. The stove rings to tell me the soufflé is ready. After a mad dash down the hallway—I discover that the soufflés have risen to perfection, a crusty golden brown.

With baguettes, fresh butter, iced Chardonnay, Perrier, salad and three kinds of salad dressing, we are ready to sit down. Bill calls everyone to the table. He has written them place cards. The table has a centerpiece of six flags—the six flags under which we have lived in the history of New Orleans.

Bill says grace, from his grab-bag box of graces. Wine and water are poured, and our celebration is complete. Around the table, the bonds of spiritual friendship are strong. Richard, sitting to my left, tells me about his Creole childhood in New Orleans. Everyone praises my soufflé, and Richard says it reminds him of one of their favorite restaurants in the south of France.

For an hour or so, there is a sense of time suspended. The clocks have stopped ticking, and we float in contentment and civility. God, it seems to us, is at the center: of who we are and the way we live and love.

Our guests have gone by three o'clock. But we move in a dream, prolonging the joy. Washing up goes easily. Carefully handling and putting away each plate or spoon gives us time with each other, to enjoy the time just spent, to relive the conversations we have had.

On Wednesday, Colette's thank-you note comes, and it's a tour de force:

The Official Gault Millau rating of Griffin's Bistro:

Le Crêpe Nanou and the Upperline, two popular uptown restaurants, ought to take heed lest Emilie Griffin, their close neighbor and noted chef, show them up. Actually, Griffin's Bistro is a family-run operation, which accounts for its consistent quality and highly personal touch. At our last visit chez Griffin's, Emilie and husband Bill turned out a French dejeuner which was pure delight. After aperitifs, guests were seated in the dining room at a table complete with white linen, international flags, crystal lamps, and a center piece of freshly baked baguettes. The main course consisted of a garden fresh salade compos, with a choice of house dressings, and a golden brown cheese soufflé. We needed only one taste of the soufflé to know that a certain bistro in Paris in the rue Tabor, which specializes in these airy concoctions, would be proud to lay claim to Emilie's ethereal creation. Complementing this was a crisp white Chardonnay. Dessert, consisting of macedoine de fruits and gateau secs, was followed by coffee and continued stimulating conversation. We wish to compliment the chef and her trusty staff for this perfectly

orchestrated summer dining experience. (Signed) Colette
H. Stelly for Christian Millau.

IN THE MIDST OF EVERYTHING, LONGING

I come at last to homewardness, a theology of my own devis-
ing, based on an experience that is commonplace, I would almost say universal. It is that kind of ordinary anguish we sometimes call homesickness and sometimes by another name, a
longing for what is not yet, a restlessness of the heart. It is an
experience so fundamentally human that, however little we
may have suffered from it ourselves (possibly some have not
confronted it, yet I suspect this yearning is embedded in their
hearts), we nevertheless find it easy to recognize and identify
with in another person. We know at once how E.T. felt when
he missed his home planet and thought he could never return.
A chord is touched in us when we hear: "E.T. phone home."

True homesickness is a very particular and limited experience which comes when things familiar and beloved are
snatched away: when the child is taken from her mother, when
the native is driven from his homeland. What follows is that
kind of exile and dislocation so often called by contemporary
writers "alienation." The writer Walker Percy speaks of the
human condition as that of a castaway. The wistful character of
America's immigrant experience and ethnic cultures may come
from this nostalgia for a lost homeland, the country idealized
in memory to which the exiles can never return.

How, on the other hand, to account for the homesickness
which has no immediate, proximate cause in our life circumstances? What about our nostalgia for something we don't fully
remember, a longing for something else, something more, not

fully focused, not entirely concrete? We sense that something is missing, something that ought to be but isn't, some fulfillment which no earthly achievement can ever furnish or supply. What we and the poets feel as something "lost" may be a memory not of the past but the future: a "memory" of something yet to be given, something that can't be fully grasped in the life we live now.

Can we build a theology on this longing for something that is not yet, a prompting that tells us we are strangers here, traveling to our home country, our rightful home? Can we build on this metaphor so deeply embedded in our poetry and our prayers? "To thee do we cry, poor banished children of Eve, to thee do we send up our sighs, mourning and weeping in this valley of tears."

This is the God we run to: the lover beyond all loves who will satisfy our deepest longing, who will nourish us with apples and cradle us in his lap. This is the God who exactly matches the God space within each of us. The answer to this inner question, this empty space, is as simple as being in love with God. The philosopher Bernard Lonergan says that such fulfillment "brings a deep-set joy that can remain despite humiliation, failure, privation, pain, betrayal, desertion. That fulfillment brings radical peace, the peace that the world cannot give."

From my own experience I would add confirming notes, corollaries to Lonergan's interpretation.

First, the "click" of recognition we feel when the idea of God is presented to us. God is a person whose nature and existence we comprehend without explanation, as though a name were being given to a being we already know. The mention of God corresponds to a longing we already know.

Second, the spontaneous flowering of belief in all times and

places, in all sorts of societies, the prevalence of the notion of
God in our speech, even in the speech of the unbeliever, an
idea which is often stamped on or thrust aside, to be sure, but
a hardy perennial nonetheless.

Third, and this is of the greatest importance, the experience
of destination which seems to gather momentum with each
passing year, so that as our physical faculties decline, we sense
ourselves moving toward an unseen goal, gathering speed, even
being quickened by the possibility of something yet to come.

There is a match between us and God. The match makes
sense. It has an inner coherence. Yet this is not the stuff for argu-
ment, for analysis. This is the stuff of the graced imagination.

It is time to pray, to put our feeble faith imagination into
play, to put ourselves in the presence of God. The older we get,
the more we know that we are in the Lord's presence already,
and to know him face to face is only a matter of time. What I
called longing or desire is really a drive, a thrust toward God,
our ultimate destiny, our destination. Faith in Lonergan's description is the experience of God's love flooding our hearts,
our unrestricted thrust to self-transcendence, our orientation
toward the mystery of love and awe. So we perceive it, not only
in the overwhelming joy of first conversion but in all the conversions of our lives, in the fervor of an intense prayer life, in
the privileged moments of our love affair with God.

But the kingdom is not yet, never fully here this side of the
boundary. Everything is a hope, a presumption, a prefiguring, a
kind of guesswork through grace. The longing remains even when
we are most aware of God, when the experience of God is embedded in our hearts. When this Lord of ours is most intensely, inti-
mately close there is still something yet to be given, an emptiness
and a hunger for what is yet to be. This love, like Shakespeare's

elusive passion, is too dear for our possessing; but again, para-
phrasing Shakespeare, it's like enough God knows his estimate.

> Wilt thou shew wonders to the dead? shall the dead arise
> and praise thee?
> Shall thy lovingkindness be declared in the grave? or
> thy faithfulness in destruction?
> Shall thy wonders be known in the dark? and thy right-
> eousness in the land of forgetfulness? (Psalm 88:10-12 KJV)

THE LAUGHTER OF RESURRECTION

One of the paintings I love is by the English artist Stanley
Spencer. It is a large oil on canvas that belongs to the Tate Gal-
lery in London. I have only seen it twice, once when it was on
loan to the Guggenheim Museum in New York, and once at
the Tate. It depicts the general resurrection and is called *The
Resurrection, Cookham.*

In this painting the moment we have all waited for is at
hand. The resurrected folk of Cookham are climbing out of
their narrow spaces, wearing the dress of various centuries as
the earth bursts into bloom. The picture is impossibly naive. So
too must we be.

Whenever I see this picture—I have a small postcard repro-
duction that is part of my devotions—I want to laugh out loud.
Resurrection is so totally absurd! I know that our human imagination cannot fully grasp it. It is beyond us; God has something
else, something far beyond our human imagination, in store.

Getting older doesn't have to be learned; it simply happens.
But to live it with grace is a kind of learning, which, like all
learning, is painful. Learning how to let go of all that has gone
before, to live memories for the sake of others instead of merely

for ourselves, to let go of mastery, to take smaller steps, to dwell in the instant, to experience the collapse of time.

"I won't be here the next time you come, Emilie," I remember as my mother-in-law's last words to me. Remembering this, I see myself standing beside the hospital bed, summoning up the will to leave her. I remember the smile, the china blue eyes, the intensity. In that moment I was swamped by her detachment, her readiness, her acceptance of what had to be. I wondered if I could ever let go so fully, so gamely, from the life I treasure as my own.

I found the same thing true with my mother. Together we moved from chair to door frame, from bath to kitchen, from bed to table, in a moment-to-moment process that prefigured my own uncertain future. Sometimes our love of theater, sometimes our playfulness sustained us as nothing else could.

"Stand up straight," I found myself telling her, "I don't want you to lose your balance. Be the Empress Helena when you enter the room." She was the leading lady. I was, at least for the moment, directing the play.

"If I am the Empress Helena," she said, "I command you to bring me a glass of ice."

And we laughed about that.

A WORD ABOUT OBSTACLES

A friend and fellow author wrote to encourage me in the completion of this book. He told me a story about how he also confronts problems of aging. When he was young, he said, he could lift 150 pounds of meat on his father's butcher blocks. Today he can scarcely lift 60 pounds of bagged sand. In fact, he was shocked to discover this. But I knew he could also see the humor in it.

I too have experienced a physical loss. I used to be a very fast walker, and now I walk slowly and with a cane. Sometimes I need assistance to go up and down steps. I push against these obstacles as much as I can. But on some level I must accept my limits.

I noticed that when our present narrative began, my mother was the one with a cane. Now she is gone, and I follow reluctantly with a cane of my own. I have invested in one or two brightly decorated canes to lend a bit of humor and lightness to this predicament. My family and I have nicknamed them. One is called "Lilac," and another one is known as "Magellan."

No question, the spiritual life is a great resource in dealing with such limitations. In my prayer I express gratitude for my life, for those who love me, for the work I can do, for the gifts the Lord has given me. One of these is a sense of humor. This kind of gratitude seems to lift me up. Gratitude expands. Gratitude strengthens me. The challenge is to live each day deeply and well, to ride the waves of experience. I pray to do that and enjoy it.

In the later years we come to see time as a gift. We open up to the life of the spirit. We deepen the present and stretch into the future. We put up more canvas to catch the winds of grace. Our souls, by God's grace, are in full sail.

JOURNEYS END IN LOVERS' MEETINGS

So I progress through the small tasks and lazinesses that mark my nights and days. In all this a relentless dialogue with the Lord continues. Words are recited silently, and these are expressions of affirmation and hope. "With your right hand you hold me, you comfort me." I hold the Lord to his word: "You prepare a table before me in the presence of my enemies. You anoint my head with oil." My prayer seems to play with the Bible language: "Only with my eyesight will I behold the reward of the wicked." I visualize, romanticize, rememorize: "For you will give your angels charge over me, to keep me in all my ways. They will bear me up in their hands, lest I dash my foot against a stone."

The voyage continues, and the destination, even though beyond us, is informed by a kind of faith confidence; we have become used to the open sea, expecting the Lord to bring us home to the place we are heading for. In the rigging somewhere we will decipher the face of Jesus Christ, or even if we do not spy him, we will know that he has gone ahead of us, the dayspring, the way-shower, the fellow sufferer who understands, God sharing our condition and transforming it. The Lord God takes hold and brings us closer to the far horizon of our future. Dawn is stealing over the rim of the world and bringing us close to fulfillment, the knowledge of who we are and where we belong.

No more will we have to be castaways. We will come home at last, in some unexplained but resolute way. I think it is something like Thor Heyerdal's raft, the Kon-Tiki, after long weeks in the Pacific swells, coming nearer to its destination. After a very long time of drifting in silence, a loud, sudden noise will shortly come from the sea birds around us, creatures who have come to tell us the dangers are over, we have come through. The moon will hang large and round; it will welcome us with a hot, even a sunlike yellow shine, even though its light is no more than a reflection of the glory yet to come. A faint, violet-blue veil over the sky will give way, by degrees, to a ruddy glow, and then, on the horizon, something like a blue pencil line.

Land.

SPIRITUAL EXERCISE

Try taking a longer view of things. Engage in some effort for the transformation of society. Churches, clubs, learned societies, groups dedicated to the handing on of tradition, all these may work to strengthen the social fabric. Perhaps, however, there is some group that is dedicated to your own vision of the good and which is pursuing it in a modest, diligent and realistic way. Whether at the level of policy or the simpler level of volunteering, seize the chance to work with them as your resources permit. "Every good gift and every perfect gift is from above, and cometh down from the Father of lights, with whom is no variableness, neither shadow of turning" (James 1:17 KJV). By involvement in the social good we act as doers of the Word, not hearers only.

QUESTIONS FOR REFLECTION

- How do you experience "living in the present moment"? (Is this more pronounced as you get older?)

- Can you think of a moment, like the Sunday brunch described in this chapter, that exemplifies this?

- Can you identify with "homewardness," the longing or yearning for fulfillment in God?

- Have you tried to imagine the general resurrection, as the painter Stanley Spencer did? Could you possibly imagine it taking place in your hometown? Or is there another place on earth that reminds you concretely of the general resurrection?

- Have you had a conversation, like Emilie's with her dying mother-in-law, that helps you connect with your own hope of resurrection?

- Is it easier, as you get older, to believe in "the glory yet to come"?

NOTES

PREFACE

p. 10   Edith as a companion and factotum: Edith Johnson, who was several years older than I, worked for my mother and for my husband and me. On the days she worked for my mother, she served essentially as a personal assistant, accompanying her both at her downtown office and at her home, helping her to handle any number of tasks—everything from housekeeping and grocery shopping to package wrapping and mailing, as well as working on various tasks for the Dietrich destination management firm. On the two days a week when she worked for us (Tuesday and Saturday), she helped us to put a full formal meal on the table at Prytania Street, often one to which our high school and college age children invited their friends. This gave a lively sense of three generations in dialogue. Edith was also a sort of mother figure to our three. She died several years ago.

p. 14   "For this is the truth about our soul": Virginia Woolf, *Mrs. Dalloway* (New York: Harcourt, Brace, 1925), p. 244. It is not Clarissa Dalloway but Peter Walsh who is speaking, but in this remarkable narrative it is always Virginia Woolf herself speaking from the depths of the soul.

p. 18   "Every current, every technique thrusts us forward": Jean Pierre de Caussade, *Abandonment to Divine Providence* (New York: Doubleday, 1975), pp. 50-51.

CHAPTER 1: SETTING OUT

p. 20   "The reason why I'm not doing so well at being old": John Churchill Chase was well known in New Orleans as a humorist, historian, cartoonist and raconteur. He is perhaps best known for his illustrated history of New Orleans, *Frenchmen Desire Good Children: And Other Streets of New Orleans*. Chase was a close friend of my parents from college days onward. He knew me as a child, but lived long enough for us to become friends as adults. He once took me to lunch at Kolb's Restaurant in New Orleans and said, "If you want to be a writer in New Orleans, you have to have your own waiter at Kolb's."

CHAPTER 2: GOOD SAILORS

pp. 28-29   United Fruit Company steamships: "The Great White Fleet" was also the name given to a fleet of steamships that operated in the First World War.

p. 30   "With my mother's death": C. S. Lewis, *Surprised by Joy: The Shape of My Early Life* (New York: Harcourt, Brace, 1955), p. 21.

pp. 30-31   "I am a product of long corridors": Ibid., p. 10.

p. 31   "And this prayer I make": William Wordsworth, "Lines Written a Few Miles Above Tintern Abbey," *Selected Poems* (New York: Penguin, 2004), p. 65.

CHAPTER 3: THE FAR HORIZON

p. 43   "God has created me": John Henry Newman, "Meditations of Christian Doctrine" (March 7), *Newman Reader* <www.newman-reader.org/works/meditations/meditations9.html>.

p. 45   desire for a "far country": I am drawing on Lewis's sermon "The Weight of Glory," preached in St. Mary the Virgin Church in Oxford in June 1941. It is published in *The Weight of Glory and Other Addresses* (Grand Rapids: Eerdmans, 1963).

p. 45   "Shall we gather at the river": Robert Lowry (1864).

p. 45   "Through all eternity you live in unapproachable light": Eucharistic Prayer IV, Roman Catholic Missal.

p. 49   Lewis showed up for a haircut unexpectedly: See William Griffin, *C. S. Lewis: The Authentic Voice* (Oxford: Lion, 2005), p. 247. My husband wrote this life of C. S. Lewis in a dramatic storytelling style. First published in 1986, it remains one of the major Lewis biographies.

p. 53   What an amazingly cheerful spirit he had: Charles Till Davis died in April 1998, just short of his sixty-ninth birthday.

CHAPTER 4: THE SPIRITUAL LIFE

p. 56   "we are converted over and over in our lives": Thomas Merton, letter to Jacques Pasquier, published in *Information Catholique Internationale,* April 1973, back cover.

p. 56   "looking through a leper's window": G. K. Chesterton, *The Catholic Church and Conversion* (New York: Macmillan, 1961), p. 64.

p. 56   "living on the ragged edge of his consciousness": William James, *The Varieties of Religious Experience* (Toronto: Macmillan, 1961), pp. 172, 177.

p. 57   "I was saying inside myself, 'Now, now, let it be now!' ": Augustine, *Confessions* bk. 8, chap. 12, trans. Rex Warner (New York: New American Library, 1963), p. 180.

p. 57   "Now I felt . . . that God was out of reach": C. S. Lewis, *Surprised by Joy* (New York: Harcourt, Brace, 1955), p. 180.

p. 58   "he calls it a powerful summons to halt and advance": Karl Barth, *Church Dogmatics* 4.2 (London: T & T Clark International, 2004), pp. 570, 574.

p. 58   "It was sea and islands now": Ibid., p. 27.

p. 59   "That night my imagination was . . . baptized": Lewis, *Surprised by Joy,* p. 181.

p. 60   the most critical moment is beginning: See my book, *Clinging: The Experience of Prayer* (Wichita, Kans.: Eighth Day Books, 2003). This is not an instructional manual but a brief work inviting the reader to experience various moods of mostly contemplative prayer.

p. 60   "we are ever but beginning": John Henry Newman, "On Christian Repentance," in *Parochial and Plain Sermons* (London: Longmans, Green, 1899), 3:90.

p. 63   "Grapple them unto thy soul with hoops of steel": William Shakespeare, *Hamlet,* act 1, scene 3, line 62, in *Shakespeare: Twenty-Three Plays and the Sonnets,* ed. Thomas Marc Parott (New York: Charles Scribner's, 1938), p. 682.

p. 66   "We are going to know a new freedom and a new happiness": "The Twelve Promises of Alcoholics Anonymous" (New York: Alcoholics Anonymous World Service, n.d.).

p. 68   "A woman with shorn white hair is standing at the kitchen window": Truman Capote, *A Christmas Memory* (New York: Random House, 1956), p. 12.

p. 69   "But I can see clear. I can see far": Emilie Griffin, *The Only Begotten Son,* unpublished playscript, 1971, p. 7.

p. 70   "a life of inner riches and spiritual freedom": Viktor E. Frankl, *Man's Search for Meaning* (New York: Washington Square Press, 1963), p. 56.

CHAPTER 5: NIGHT FEARS

p. 77   "Kate sat under the tree in such a way": Doris Lessing, *The Summer Before the Dark* (New York: Bantam Books, 1978), p. 8.

p. 86   "The mind is its own place, and in itself": John Milton, *Paradise Lost,* book 1, lines 254-55, in *The Complete Poetical Works of John Milton,* ed. Henry Francis Fletcher (Boston: Houghton Mifflin, 1941), p. 160. Milton attributes this remark to Beelzebub, but it is commonly taken to be something Milton himself believed to be true.

CHAPTER 6: CHURCHYARDS

p. 98   "You know as well as I do": Thornton Wilder, *Our Town* (New York: Harper & Row Perennial Library, 1957), p. 82.

p. 98   "At last to be identified!": Emily Dickinson, "Resurgam," in *Favorite Poems of Emily Dickinson* (New York: Avenel Books, 1978), p. 141.

p. 99 "They are all gone into the world of light": Henry Vaughan, "They Are All Gone into That World of Light," in *Seventeenth-Century Prose and Poetry*, ed. Alexander M. Witherspoon and Frank J. Warnke (New York: Harcourt, Brace and World, 1963), pp. 985-86.

p. 100 "Jerusalem, Jerusalem, lift up your gates and sing!" F. E. Weatherly, "Holy City" (1944).

p. 100 "Who's that yonder, dressed in red": John W. Work Jr., "Go Tell It on the Mountain" (1907).

p. 101 St. Francisville, Louisiana, is treated as an image of heaven in my book *Chasing the Kingdom* (San Francisco: HarperSanFrancisco, 1990). I was influenced to do this by Stanley Spencer's painting "The Resurrection: Cookham." He depicts the general resurrection in his home village of Cookham, Surrey, England.

p. 102 The novelist Walker Percy: My long visit with Walker Percy and his wife took place at their home in Covington, Louisiana, on July 23, 1981. On that occasion Walker Percy inscribed a copy of his novel *Lancelot* and gave it to me.

p. 105 "Then again, her thoughts would drift into places": Eleanor Munro, "A Pilgrimage Renews a Life: Mother and Daughter and Memory," *New York Times*, July 11, 1993, p. 41.

CHAPTER 7: WEAVING FAMILY RITUALS

p. 109 "White? It means nothing to me": Interview with Robert McGriff, in "Together Apart: The Myth of Race," part 3, *Times Picayune*, August 16, 1993, p. 1.

p. 118 "The Bible everywhere encourages us to believe": John Baillie, *Invitation to Pilgrimage* (Harmondsworth, U.K.: Penguin Books, 1960), p. 126.

p. 119 "We can count on having God on our side": Ibid., p. 127.

p. 122 "What shall I give him, poor that I am?": Christina Rossetti, "A Christmas Carol," in *Spiritual Classics*, ed. Richard J. Foster and Emilie Griffin (San Francisco: HarperSanFrancisco, 2000), pp. 309-10.

p. 125 the prayer of Ebenezer Scrooge: Charles Dickens, *A Christmas Carol* (New York: Holiday House, 1983), pp. 105-6.

p. 125 "Generative care is able to let go": Evelyn Eaton Whitehead and James D. Whitehead, *Christian Life Patterns* (New York: Crossroad, 1992), p. 130.

CHAPTER 8: A DIFFERENT WISDOM

p. 128 "The Cross comes before the crown": C. S. Lewis, *The Weight of Glory and Other Addresses* (Grand Rapids: Eerdmans, 1975), p. 14.

p. 138 "Growing older is a phenomenon which is a common denominator for all of us": Marie Lenihan, "Taking Life's Walk with the Elderly," Brooklyn Tablet, date unknown.

p. 139   "Sunset, and evening star": Alfred, Lord Tennyson, "Crossing the Bar," in *England in Literature*, ed. Robert C. Pooley et al. (Chicago: Scott Foresman, 1953), p. 401.

CHAPTER 9: EASTERING

p. 141   "Let him easter in us": Gerard Manley Hopkins, "The Wreck of the Deutchland," in *Gerard Manley Hopkins: Poetry and Prose* (Harmondsworth, U.K.: Penguin Books, 1963), p. 24.

p. 142   "I admire thee, master of the tides": Ibid., p. 23.

p. 143   eighteen-year-old man in the Mayo Clinic: See James McKay, *The Management of Time* (Englewood Cliffs, N.J.: Prentice-Hall, 1959), pp. 71-75.

p. 150   "the focus of your interests becomes pinpoint-precise": Armand Hammer, *Hammer* (New York: G. P. Putnam's, 1987), p. 468.

p. 151   Janice Brewi and wisdom rooted in religious experience: Janice Brewi and Anne Brennan, *Celebrate Mid-Life* (New York: Crossroad, 1988).

p. 151   "God awaits us every instant in our action": Teilhard de Chardin, *The Divine Milieu* (New York: Harper & Row, 1960), quoted in ibid., pp. 248-49.

p. 152   "We must be active in all that the present moment demands": Jean-Pierre de Caussade, *Abandonment to Divine Providence*, trans. John Beevers (New York: Doubleday, 1975), p. 79.

p. 153   Christ can be a "dayspring to the dimness in us": Hopkins, "Wreck of the Deutschland," p. 24.

p. 155   "Because I could not stop for death": Emily Dickinson, "The Chariot," in *Favorite Poems of Emily Dickinson* (New York: Avenel Books, 1978), p. 138.

CHAPTER 10: HOMEWARD

p. 171   "To thee do we cry, poor banished children of Eve": from "Hail Holy Queen," is sung from Trinity Sunday until the Saturday before the first Sunday of Advent in the Roman Catholic Church.

p. 171   such fulfillment "brings a deep-set joy": Bernard J. F. Lonergan, *Method in Theology* (New York: Seabury Press, 1972), pp. 103, 105.

p. 173   This love, like Shakespeare's elusive passion: See William Shakespeare, Sonnet 87, lines 1-2, in *The Sonnets of William Shakespeare*. The lines read: "Farewell, thou art too dear for my possessing / And like enough thou know'st thine estimate."